THE LITTLE FLOWERS
OF SAINT FRANCIS ❧

OF ASSISI ❧ WITH EIGHT
ILLUSTRATIONS BY PAUL
WOODROFFE ❧ ❧ ❧ ❧

LONDON: KEGAN PAUL · TRENCH
TRÜBNER AND COMPANY LIMITED
MDCCCCV ❧ ❧ ❧ ❧ ❧

Prefatory Note

THIS edition of the *Fioretti* is based by permission upon the translation issued by the Franciscan Fathers at Upton, which has been for some time out of print. It has been carefully revised by Mr. Thomas Okey, and when necessary has been brought into closer accordance with the Italian, care having been taken to preserve as much as possible the simplicity of the original. The present publishers are enabled to avail themselves of so scholarly a rendering by the courtesy of the Catholic Truth Society, under whose auspices it first appeared. The compiler of the *Fioretti* is unknown, but the work is supposed to date from the middle of the fourteenth century.

512133

CONTENTS

Contents

THE LITTLE
FLOWERS OF
ST FRANCIS

IN the name of our Lord Jesus Christ crucified, and of His Virgin Mother Mary.
In this book are contained certain little
Flowers, namely, miracles and devout
examples of the glorious poor little one
of Christ, St Francis, and of some of
his holy companions, to the praise of
Jesus Christ. Amen.

In the first place, let us consider how
the glorious St Francis, in all the acts of
his life, was conformed to the life of that
blessed Christ; that, as Christ in the beginning of His preaching elected twelve
apostles, that they should despise every
worldly thing and follow Him in poverty
and in all virtues, so St Francis, for the
founding of his order, elected in the beginning twelve companions, who were to be
possessors of nothing but an entire poverty.
And as one of the twelve apostles of Christ,
rejected by God for his infidelity, finally
strangled himself, so also one of the twelve
companions of St Francis, who was called
Brother John della Capella, apostatized,
and finally hanged himself in like manner.
And this is to the elect a great warning,
and a matter of humility and of fear, to

B

cause them to remember that no one is certain to persevere to the end in the grace of God. As the blessed apostles were wholly marvellous for sanctity and humility and full of the Holy Ghost, so the blessed companions of St Francis were men of such great sanctity that since the time of the apostles, the world had not seen the like; since one of them, like St Paul, was taken up into the third heaven, and this was Brother Giles; another of them, namely Brother Filippo Longo, was touched on the lips by an angel, like the Prophet Isaias, with a coal of fire; another of them, and this was Brother Silvester, spoke with God, as one friend with another, after the manner of Moses; another, by the purity of his soul, flew up to the light of the Divine Wisdom, like the eagle, St John the Evangelist, and this was the most humble Brother Bernard, who explained most profoundly Holy Writ; and another was sanctified by God and canonized in heaven whilst still living on earth, and this was Brother Ruffino, who was a gentleman of Assisi. And so were they all privileged with remarkable signs of holiness, as will be declared in the sequel.

I—Of Brother Bernard, First Companion of St Francis

THE first companion of St Francis was Brother Bernard of Assisi, who was converted in the following manner. While St Francis

was still in the secular habit, although he
had already turned his back on the world
▸going about wholly despised of men, morti-
fied by penance insomuch that he was
looked upon as a fool by many and, as he
passed by, was driven away with stones and
foul abuse both by his relatives and by
others, all of which ill-usage and contumely
he bore patiently as though he were deaf
and dumb; Bernard of Assisi, who was one
of the richest, and most noble, and most
learned in all the town, began wisely to consider within himself the great patience of
St Francis under ill-treatment, and his so
exceeding contempt of the world, insomuch
that, detested and despised as he was by
everybody now for the space of two years,
he only appeared the more firm. Then he
began thus to think and to say within himself: " It cannot be otherwise, but that this
brother must have great grace from God ; "
and he invited him one evening to sup with
him, and to pass the night. St Francis accepted the invitation, and took supper with
him, and stayed the night also; and then
Bernard resolved to make trial of his sanctity. Wherefore he got a bed prepared for
him in his own room, in which a lamp was
always burning all night. St Francis, in
order to conceal his sanctity, immediately
on entering the room threw himself on the
bed, and feigned to sleep; and Bernard likewise resolved to lie down, and began to snore
loudly, as if in a very deep slumber.

Thereupon St Francis, believing that Bernard was really asleep, immediately rose from the bed and betook himself to prayer; and raising his eyes and his hands to heaven with the greatest devotion and fervour, he said, " My God, my God ! " So saying, and shedding many tears, he remained until morning, continually repeating " My God, my God ! " and nothing more. And this he said, contemplating and admiring the excellency of the Divine Majesty, which deigned to stoop down to the world that was perishing, and to provide a remedy for the salvation of his soul, and through him—His poor little Francis—for the salvation of the souls of others. Then, illumined by the Holy Ghost with the spirit of prophecy to foresee the great things that God designed to do through him and through his order, and considering his own insufficiency and how little virtue was in himself, he called upon God, and besought Him that through His goodness and omnipotence He would supply help and perfect that which human frailty could not do of itself.

Bernard, seeing by the light of the lamp these most devout acts of St Francis, and devoutly within himself considering also the words which he heard him say, was touched and inspired by the Holy Ghost to change his life. In the morning therefore he called St Francis, and spoke to him thus: " Brother Francis, I have completely disposed my heart to give up the world, and to follow thee

in what thou shalt command me." Hearing
this, St Francis rejoiced in spirit, and answered : " Bernard, that which you speak
about is a work so great and important, that
we must ask advice in it from our Lord Jesus
Christ, and beg of Him that it may please
Him to show us His will concerning it, and
to teach us how we shall be able to put it
into execution ; and therefore let us go together to the bishop's house, where there is
a good priest, and let us have Mass said;
then we shall remain in prayer until terce,
beseeching God that by our three times
opening the missal, He will show us the way
which it pleases Him that we should choose."
Bernard replied that this pleased him very
much.

They started, therefore, and went to the
bishop's house, and after hearing Mass, and
remaining in prayer until terce, the priest, at
the request of St Francis, took the missal,
and having made the sign of the most holy
cross, he opened it three times in the name
of our Lord Jesus Christ.

At the first opening appeared these
words, which our Lord said to the young
man who asked about the way to perfection :
" If thou wilt be perfect, go, sell what thou
hast, and give to the poor, and follow Me."
(St Matt. xix. 21.) At the second opening
appeared these words, which Christ spoke
to the apostles when He sent them to
preach : " Take nothing for your journey,
neither staff, nor scrip, nor bread, nor

money " (St Luke ix. 3); wishing by this to teach them that all their dependence should be placed in God, and their whole attention turned to the teaching of the Holy Gospel. At the third opening of the missal appeared these other words, which Christ said : " If any man will follow Me, let him deny himself, and take up his cross, and follow Me." (St Mark xiii. 34.) Then St Francis said to Bernard : " Behold the advice which Christ gives; go then and accomplish what you have read ; and blessed be our Lord Jesus Christ, who has deigned to show us the way to live in accordance with His Gospel."

Having read this, Bernard departed, and sold all he had (and he was very rich), and with great joy he distributed everything to the sick, and to widows and orphans and prisoners, and to monasteries, hospices and pilgrims ; and in all things St Francis helped him faithfully and wisely. And one Silvester, seeing that St Francis distributed, and caused to be distributed, so much money to the poor, being moved by avarice, said to St Francis: " You did not pay me enough for those stones which you purchased from me for the repairs of the church ; seeing that now you have money, therefore pay me." Then St Francis, astonished at his avarice, and as a true observer of the Holy Gospel not wishing to dispute with him, put his hands into the sack of Bernard, and filled them with coins which he placed in the sack

of Silvester, saying that if he wished more
he would give him more.

Silvester, satisfied with this, departed and
went home. But in the evening, reflecting on
what he had done through the day, and
blaming himself on account of his avarice,
considering the fervour of Bernard and the
sanctity of St Francis—on that night and
the two following nights he had from God
this vision : that from the mouth of St
Francis there issued a golden cross, the top
of which touched heaven, and the arms
extended from the east to the west.
Touched by this vision he gave away for the
love of God all that he possessed, and became
a Friar Minor, and lived in the order in so
great holiness and grace, that he spoke with
God as one friend does with another, as St
Francis frequently witnessed, and as will be
explained more fully later on. Bernard
likewise had such great grace from God, that
he was frequently rapt in contemplation by
the power of God, and St Francis said of
him that he was worthy of all reverence, and
that it was he who had founded the order,
because he was the first who had given up
the world, and begun the life of evangelical
poverty, reserving nothing for himself, but
giving everything to the poor of Christ, and
placing himself naked in the arms of the
Crucified, whom may we bless for ever and
ever. Amen.

II—How St Francis, on account of an un-
charitable thought which he had concerning Brother Bernard, commanded the said
Brother that he should tread three times
on his throat and mouth

ST FRANCIS, that most devout servant of the
Crucified, through the rigour of his penance
and by continual weeping, had almost lost
his sight, and become nearly blind. It came
to pass on one occasion that he departed
from the place where he was, and went to the
place where Brother Bernard was, to speak
with him about divine things; and having
arrived at the place, he found Brother
Bernard in a wood, wholly raised up and
united to God in prayer. Then St Francis,
going into the wood, called him: " Come,"
he said, " and speak with this blind man."
And Brother Bernard answered him not,
because, he being a man of deep contemplation, his mind was suspended above
the earth and raised up to God. Now because
this brother had a singular grace in speaking of God, as St Francis had often proved,
he desired the more to speak with him :
therefore after some time, he called him a
second and a third time, after the same
manner; but neither then did Brother
Bernard hear him, nor, consequently, did he
come to him or give him any answer.
Thereupon St Francis departed a little disconsolate, marvelling within himself and

fretting because Brother Bernard, being called three times, did not come to him.

Therefore departing with this thought, St Francis, when he had gone a little way, said to his companion: "Wait here for me;" and he went to a solitary place hard by, and prostrated himself in prayer, begging of God that He would reveal to him why Brother Bernard did not answer him. And as he prayed, there came to him a voice from God, which said: "O thou poor miserable little man, why art thou thus troubled? Should a man leave God for a creature? Brother Bernard, when thou calledst him, was communing with Me, and therefore was not able to go to thee, nor to answer thee, seeing that he was so much out of himself that he heard none of thy words." Then St Francis, having got this answer from God, immediately returned to Brother Bernard, in great grief, to accuse himself humbly of the thoughts which he had had concerning him.

And seeing St Francis coming towards him, Brother Bernard went to meet him, and threw himself at his feet. But St Francis bade him arise, and told him, with great humility, the thought he had had, the trouble in his mind concerning him, and in what manner God had replied to him; and he concluded thus: "I command thee by holy obedience to do that which I shall command thee." Then Brother Bernard, fearing that St Francis would command him to do something excessive, as was his wont, and wishing, without fault, to escape this obedience, answered him: "I am ready to do this obedience, if thou wilt promise me also to do that which I shall command thee." And St Francis having promised him, he said: "Now say, father, what it is that thou wishest me to do." Then St Francis said to him: "I command thee, under holy obedience, that in order to punish my presumption and the rashness of my heart, when I shall cast myself down on the ground, thou shalt put one foot on my throat and the other on my mouth, and then pass over me three times from one side to the other, speaking to me reproachfully and contemptuously, and especially saying to me: 'Lie there, miserable little son of Peter Bernardone; whence comes to thee so much pride, seeing thou art a most vile creature?'"

Hearing this, Brother Bernard, although it went very hard with him to do it, yet, through holy obedience, performed as gently as possible that which St Francis had commanded. And when he had done so, St Francis said: "Now command thou me that which thou wouldst have me to do for thee, seeing that I have promised thee obedience." And Brother Bernard said: "I command thee, by holy obedience, that every time we are together thou shalt reprove me for my defects and correct them sharply." At this St Francis marvelled greatly, inasmuch as Brother Bernard was of such great sanctity that he held him in great reverence, and did

not deem him blameworthy in anything; and
therefore from that time forward St Francis
took care not to stay much with him, on
account of the said obedience, so that no
word of correction might come from him
towards one whom he knew to be of such
great holiness. But when he wanted to see
him or to hear him speak about God, as soon
as possible he left him again, and departed;
and it was of the greatest edification to see
with what charity and reverence and
humility the Father St Francis acted and
spoke to Brother Bernard, his first-born son.
To the praise and glory of Jesus Christ, and
of the poor little one, St Francis. Amen.

III—How the Angel of God proposed a question to Brother Elias, and because Brother
Elias replied to him haughtily, departed,
and went along the road to San Giacomo,
where Brother Bernard was, and told him
this story

IN the beginning, at the commencement of
the order, when there were few brothers,
and the houses* were not numerous, St
Francis went out of devotion to St James's
of Galicia,† taking with him a few brothers,
among whom was Brother Bernard. And
as they went together along the road, they

---

* Meaning the Franciscan settlements or convents.
† The Cathedral of Compostella, in Spain.

found a poor little sick man; and having compassion on him, St Francis said to Brother Bernard : " My little son, I wish that thou shouldst remain here, to take care of this sick man;" and Brother Bernard, humbly throwing himself on his knees and inclining his head, received the obedience of the holy father, and remained in that place, while St Francis with his other companions went on to St James's. Having arrived there, St Francis remained all the night in prayer in the church of St James; and it was revealed to him by God that he should take possession of many places throughout the world, because his order would increase, and grow to a great multitude of brothers; and when this was revealed to him, St Francis began in his mind to fix upon places in all these countries.

Then St Francis returned by the same way as he had come, and found Brother Bernard and the sick man with whom he had left him, who was now perfectly healed. Wherefore, in the next year, St Francis gave permission to Brother Bernard to go to St James's. And St Francis returned to the valley of Spoleto, and took up his abode there in a solitary place; himself and Brother Masseo, and Brother Elias, and some others, all of whom took great care not to disturb or distract St Francis at prayer; and this they did for the great reverence they bore him, and because they knew that God revealed great things to him in his prayer.

It happened one day that, St Francis
being in prayer in a wood, a fair youth,
dressed as a traveller, came to the door of the
convent, and knocked with such haste and
loudness, and for so long a time, that the
brothers wondered greatly at such an un-
usual knocking. Brother Masseo therefore
went to the door, and said : " Whence come
you, my little son, for it does not seem you
have been here before, seeing you have not
knocked according to custom ? "   The youth
replied : " And how must I knock ? "   Brother Masseo said : " Give three knocks, one
after the other, with a pause between each;
then wait till the brother has said a Pater
noster, and if in this space he does not
come, knock again."   The youth replied :
" I am in great haste, and therefore I knock
so loudly, because I have to make a journey,
and I have come to speak to Brother Francis;
but he is now in the wood, in contemplation,
and therefore I do not wish to disturb him ;
but go and tell Brother Elias from me, that
I wish to propose a question to him, because
I have heard that he is very learned."   So
Brother Masseo went and told Brother Elias
to go to the youth ; but he was annoyed at
it, and did not wish to do so. Therefore
Brother Masseo did not know what to do,
nor what answer to give ; because if he
had said that Brother Elias could not
come, it would have been a lie, and if
he had said that he was so much annoyed,
and that he would not come, he was

afraid of giving bad example to the youth.

And while the brother delayed, thinking what to do, the youth knocked again, and a little more persistently ; so Brother Masseo returned to the door, and said to the youth : "You have not yet observed my lesson in knocking." The youth replied : "Brother Elias does not wish to come to me ; but go and tell Brother Francis that I came to speak to him, but as I do not wish to hinder him from prayer, tell him to send Brother Elias to me." Then Brother Masseo went to Brother Francis, where he was praying in the wood with his face raised towards heaven, and told him the message of the youth, and the reply of Brother Elias. Now this youth was an angel of God in human form. Then St. Francis, without moving from his place or turning his face downwards, said to Brother Masseo : "Go and tell Brother Elias to go immediately, under obedience, to this youth."

Brother Elias, receiving the obedience of St. Francis, went to the door, greatly disturbed, and opened it with a great push and much noise, and said to the youth : "What do you want ?" The youth answered : "Take care, brother, that you be not disturbed, as you appear to be, because anger troubles the soul, and does not allow it to perceive the truth." Brother Elias said again : "Tell me what you want of me." Then the youth said : " I ask thee is it lawful

for observers of the Holy Gospel to eat that
which is put before them, according to what
Christ said to His disciples; and I ask thee
again, if it is lawful for any man to lay down
aught that is contrary to the liberty of the
Gospel." But Brother Elias answered him
laughingly: "I know well, but I do not
wish to answer you; go about your business."
The youth said : " I could answer that question better than you." Then Brother Elias
was angry, and shut the door in a rage, and
departed.

Afterwards, he began to think about this
question, and to doubt about it within himself, and he could not solve it; because he
was vicar of the order, and had made a
constitution going beyond the Gospel and
the rule of St Francis, that no brother
should eat meat; so that the said question
was aimed expressly against him. Therefore, not knowing how to explain it, and
considering the modesty of the youth, and
that he said he could answer the question
better than himself, he returned to the door,
and opened it again intending to ask the
youth about the same question; but he was
already gone, because the pride of Brother
Elias was unworthy to speak with an angel.
This done, St Francis, to whom the whole
had been revealed by God, turned towards
Brother Elias in the wood, and with a loud
voice strongly rebuked him, saying: " Ill
done, proud Brother Elias; thou hast driven
away the holy angel who came here to teach

us. I tell thee, I fear greatly that thy pride will make thee end thy days outside this order." And so it happened to him afterwards, as St Francis had told him, for he died outside of the order.

On the same day and in the same hour that he departed from his place, the angel appeared in the same form to Brother Bernard, who was returning from St James's, and was by the bank of a great river, and saluted him in his own language, saying: "God give thee peace, O good brother!" And the good Brother Bernard marvelled greatly, and considering the comeliness of the youth, and the language of his country, together with his wishing him peace, and his joyful countenance, he asked him: "Whence comest thou, good youth?" The angel replied: "I come from the place where St Francis lives, and I went there to speak with him, and I could not, because he was in the wood contemplating things divine, and I did not wish to disturb him. And in that place, Brother Masseo and Brother Giles, and Brother Elias live; and Brother Masseo taught me how to knock at the door like the brothers: but Brother Elias, because he did not wish to answer the question I proposed to him, afterwards repented, and wished to hear me and see me, but he could not."

After these words, the angel said to Brother Bernard: "Wherefore dost thou not cross over?" Brother Bernard replied:

"Because I fear the danger, on account of the depth of the water that I see." And the angel said : " Let us cross together and have no fear ; " and he took his hand, and in the twinkling of an eye placed him on the other side of the river. And then Brother Bernard knew that he was an angel of God, and with great reverence and joy, with a loud voice he said : " O blessed angel of God ! tell me, what is thy name ? " The angel replied : " Wherefore askest thou my name, which is Marvellous ? " And having said this, the angel disappeared and left Brother Bernard much consoled ; so much so, that he performed the whole journey with great joy, and he took note of the day and the hour that the angel had appeared to him. And arriving at the place where St Francis was with his companions above-named, he told him the whole story in order, and they knew with certainty that the same angel on that day, and in that hour, had appeared both to them and to him.

IV—How the holy Brother Bernard of Assisi was sent by St Francis to Bologna, and there founded a House

As St Francis and his companions were called and elected by God to carry in heart, and to preach in word and in work, the cross of Christ; and as, both in appearance, by reason of the habit which they wore, and in fact, by reason of their austere life and

c

their acts and conduct, they were crucified
men, therefore they desired the more to
undergo shame and contumely for the love
of Christ, rather than to receive the honours
of the world, or the reverence and praises of
men. They rejoiced in ill-treatment, they
were sad in honours; and so they went
through the world, as strangers and pilgrims,
taking nothing with them but Christ
crucified. And because they were true
branches of the true Vine, they produced
great and good fruit of souls, which they
gained to God.

It happened in the beginning of the
order, that St Francis sent Brother Bernard
to Bologna, that there, according to the
grace that God had given him, he should
bear fruit unto God; and Brother Bernard,
making the sign of the most holy cross,
through holy obedience set out and arrived
at Bologna. And the children, seeing him
in a strange and poor habit, offered him
many insults and much ill-treatment, as they
would have done to a fool; and Brother
Bernard patiently and joyfully bore everything for the love of Christ; and in order to
receive the more ill-treatment, he went out
purposely to the piazza of the city. There
many children and men came about him,
and some pulled his hood from behind and
some from before; others, in front, threw
dust and stones upon him, and others pushed
him from side to side; and Brother Bernard,
always in the same manner, and with the

same patience, and with a joyful countenance, neither got annoyed nor troubled; and for many days he returned to this place, to undergo the like treatment.

And as patience is a work of perfection and a proof of virtue, a doctor learned in the law, seeing and considering within himself the great constancy of Brother Bernard, and how he was not disturbed during so many days by any contumely and ill-treatment, said within himself: "It is impossible that this should not be a holy man;" and approaching him, he asked him: "Who art thou? and wherefore hast thou come here?" And Brother Bernard for reply put his hand in his breast, and drew out the rule of St Francis, and gave it to him to read. And he having read it, and considering its most sublime state of perfection with the greatest astonishment and admiration, turned to his companions and said: "Verily, this is the highest state of religion I have ever heard of; therefore this man and his companions are the holiest men in the world, and he who illtreats him commits a very great sin; for he should rather be highly honoured, considering that he is a dear friend of God." And he said to Brother Bernard: "If you wish for a house where you can peacefully serve God, I will willingly give it to you, for the salvation of my soul." Brother Bernard replied: " Sir, I believe that our Lord Jesus Christ has inspired you with this thought; and as for your offer, I accept it willingly for the honour of Christ." Then this lawyer, with great joy and love, conducted Brother Bernard to his house; and then he gave over to him the promised dwelling, with all its furniture, fitted up at his own charge; and from that day he became the father and special defender of Brother Bernard and his companions.

And Brother Bernard, by reason of his holy manner of life, began to be much honoured by the people, insomuch that blessed did he esteem himself, who could touch him or see him; but he, as a true disciple of Christ and of the humble Francis, fearing lest the honours of the world should hinder the peace and salvation of his soul, departed one day, and returned to St Francis, and spoke thus : " Father, the house is founded near to the city of Bologna ; command the brothers that they maintain it, and that they stay there; for I have no more profit there, because of the too great honour which is paid to me ; for I fear lest I should lose more than I gain." Then St Francis, hearing all these things, and how God had worked by Brother Bernard, returned thanks to God, who had thus begun and increased the number of the poor little disciples of the cross. And then he sent forth some of his companions to Bologna and to Lombardy, who founded houses in various parts.

V—How St Francis blessed the holy Brother
Bernard, and appointed him his Vicar,
when the time came for him to pass
away from this life

BROTHER BERNARD was of so high a degree of sanctity that St Francis bore him a
great reverence, and constantly spoke in his
praise. It happened one day that, while St.
Francis was devoutly praying, it was revealed to him from God that Brother Bernard, by the divine permission, should
sustain many and severe combats with the
demons, at which St Francis, having great
compassion for the said Brother Bernard,
whom he loved as his own son, prayed with
tears for many days, entreating God for him,
and recommending him to our Lord Jesus
Christ, that He might give him the victory
over the demon. And as St Francis prayed
thus devoutly one day, God made answer to
him : " Francis, fear not, for all the temptations by which this Brother Bernard must
be assailed are permitted of God, for the
exercise of his virtue and the crowning of
his merits; and finally, he shall have the
victory over his enemies, for that he is one
of the chosen ones of the kingdom of heaven." At which answer, St Francis had
the greatest joy, and returned thanks to God,
and from that same hour he bore him still
greater love and reverence. And this was
shown not only in his life but at his death.

For the hour of his death having come, and having, like the holy patriarch Jacob, his devoted sons standing around him, sorrowing and weeping at parting from so loving a father, he asked : "Where is my first-born ? Come to me, my son, that my soul may bless thee before I die." Then Brother Bernard said secretly to Brother Elias, who was vicar of the order : " Father, go to the right hand of the saint, that he may bless thee." And Brother Elias, placing himself at his right hand, St Francis, who had lost his sight through his many tears, placed his right hand on the head of Brother Elias, and said : " This is not the head of my first-born, Brother Bernard." Then Brother Bernard went to him, on his left hand, and St Francis, placing his arms in the form of the cross, laid his right hand on the head of Brother Bernard, and his left on that of Brother Elias, and said to Brother Bernard : " God, the Father of our Lord Jesus Christ, bless thee with all spiritual and heavenly blessings, inasmuch as thou art the first-born, chosen in this holy order, to give the evangelical example, and to follow Christ in evangelical poverty, seeing that not only didst thou part with all that was thine, and give with zeal and generosity to the poor, for the love of Christ, but thou didst offer thyself also to God in this order, for a sacrifice of sweetness. Bblessed be thou, therefore, of our Lord Jesus Christ, and of me, His poor little servant, with an

eternal blessing, going and coming, waking
and sleeping, living and dying ; whosoever
doth bless thee shall be replenished with
blessings, and he that would curse thee shall
not go unpunished.   Be thou first among
thy brethren, and to thy commands let all
the brethren be obedient ; have thou licence
to receive into this order whom thou wilt,
and let no brother be lord over thee, but be
thou free to God to come as it shall please
thee."

And after the death of St Francis, the
brothers loved and reverenced Brother Bernard as a venerable father.   And when he
came to die, there came to him many brothers from divers parts of the world, amongst
whom came that angelic and divine Brother
Giles, who looking at Brother Bernard with
great joy, said to him: "*Sursum corda*,
Brother Bernard, *sursum corda*."   And Brother Bernard said secretly to one of the
brothers that they should prepare for Brother Giles a suitable lodging, wherein he
might give himself to heavenly contemplation ; and this was done.

Then Brother Bernard, being come to the
last hour of his life, had himself raised up,
and spoke to the brothers who stood around
him, saying: " Most beloved brothers, I will
not speak many words to you ; but you must
consider that the religious state which has
been mine, is still yours, and the hour which
has now come for me, will come for you also :
and I find this within my soul, that for a

thousand worlds equal to this present one,
I would not have served any other master
than our Lord Jesus Christ; and for all
offences which I have committed, I accuse
myself, and ask pardon of my Saviour Jesus,
and of you. I beg you my most dear brothers, that you continue to love one another."
And after these words, and other good instructions, he laid himself down in his bed :
and his face grew resplendent, and joyful
beyond measure, so that all the brothers
marvelled exceedingly, and in this rapture
of his holy soul, crowned with glory, passed
from this present life to the blessed life of
the angels.

VI—How St Francis passed the Lent in an
island in the Lake of Perugia, where he
fasted forty days and forty nights

THE true servant of Christ, St Francis, was
in some sense as another Christ, given to
the world for the salvation of the people ;
therefore God the Father willed to make him
in many of his actions conformable to the
image of His Son, Jesus Christ. This was
shown in the venerable company of his
twelve companions, and in the admirable
mystery of the sacred stigmata, and in his
continuous fast during the holy Lent, which
took place in this manner.

Once on a time, St Francis on the day
of the carnival went to the Lake of Perugia,
to the house of one of his disciples, where

he was entertained for the night, and there
he was inspired by God to pass this Lent on
an island in the lake. Wherefore St Francis
prayed his disciple, that for the love of Christ
he would carry him across in his little boat
to an island in the lake where no one
inhabited, and that he would do this on the
night of Ash Wednesday, so that no one
might know of it. Then the other, for the
great love and devotion he bore to St
Francis, solicitous to grant his request,
carried him to the said island, and St Francis
took nothing with him but two little loaves.

And when they had arrived at the island,
and his friend was about to return to his
home, St Francis earnestly besought him
not to reveal to any one what he should do,
and not to come again till Holy Thursday.
So his friend departed, and St Francis
remained alone; and there being no hal.i-
tation into which he could retire, he entered
into a thicket, where many trees and shrubs
had formed a hiding-place, resembling a
little hut : and in this shelter he disposed
himself to prayer and to the contemplation
of heavenly things.

And he remained there the whole of Lent,
without eating or drinking, except the half
of one of those little loaves, as was witnessed
by his disciple when he returned to him on
Holy Thursday, who found, of the two loaves,
one entire, and the half of the other. It is
believed that St Francis so refrained from
eating out of reverence for the fasting of the

blessed Christ, who fasted forty days and
forty nights without taking any material
food ; and thus with that half loaf he kept
from himself the poison of vainglory, and
after the example of Christ he fasted forty
days and forty nights.

And afterwards, in this spot, where St
Francis had sustained this marvellous
abstinence, God granted many miracles
through his merits; for which cause men
began to build houses there, and to inhabit
them ; and in a short time there was built a
large and prosperous village, and the house
for the brothers, which is still called the
House of the Island. And to this day the
men and women of the village have great
reverence and devotion for the spot where
St Francis made this Lent.

VII—How St Francis showed to Brother Leo
    what are the things in which consists
    perfect joy

As St Francis went once on a time from
Perugia to St. Mary of the Angels with
Brother Leo, in the winter, they suffered
greatly from the severity of the cold, and St
Francis called to Brother Leo, who was going
on a little in advance: " O Brother Leo,
although the Friars Minor in these parts give
a great example of sanctity and good edification, write it down and note it well that this
is not perfect joy." And having gone a little
further, he called to him the second time :

"O Brother Leo, even though the Friars Minor should give sight to the blind, and loose the limbs of the paralysed, and though they should cast out devils, and give hearing to the deaf, speech to the dumb and the power of walking to the lame, and although—which is a greater thing than these—they should raise to life those who had been dead four days, write that in all this there is not perfect joy." And going on a little while, he cried aloud : "O Brother Leo, if the Friars Minor knew all languages and all the sciences and all the Scriptures, and if they could prophesy and reveal not only things in the future, but the secrets of consciences and of men's souls, write that in all this there it not perfect joy." Going still a little further, St Francis called aloud again : "O Brother Leo, thou little sheep of God, even though the Friars Minor spoke with the tongues of angels, and knew the courses of the stars, and the virtue of herbs, and though to them were revealed all the treasures of the earth, and that they knew the virtues of birds and of fishes and of all animals and of men, of trees also and of stones and roots and waters, write that not in this is perfect joy." And going yet a little while on the way, St Francis called aloud: "O Brother Leo, even though the Friars Minor should preach so well that they should convert all the infidels to the faith of Christ, write that herein is not perfect joy."

And as he spoke in this manner during

two good miles, Brother Leo in great astonishment asked of him, and said: "Father,
I pray thee, for God's sake, tell me wherein
is perfect joy." And St Francis replied to
him: "When we shall have come to St
Mary of the Angels, soaked as we are with
the rain and frozen with the cold, encrusted
with mud and afflicted with hunger, and
shall knock at the door, if the porter should
come and ask angrily, 'Who are you?' and
we replying: 'We are two of your brethren,'
he should say: 'You speak falsely; you are
two good-for-nothings, who go about the
world stealing alms from the poor; go your
way;' and if he would not open the door to
us, but left us without, exposed till night to
the snow and the wind and the torrents of
rain, in cold and hunger; then, if we should
bear so much abuse and cruelty and such a
dismissal patiently, without disturbance
and without murmuring at him, and should
think humbly and charitably that this porter knew us truly, and that God would have
him speak against us, O Brother Leo, write
that this would be perfect joy. And if we
should continue to knock, and he should
come out in a rage, and should drive us
away as importunate villains, with rudeness
and with buffetings, saying: 'Depart from
this house, vile thieves; go to the poor-
house, for you shall neither eat nor be lodged
here;' if we should sustain this with patience, and with joy, and with love, O Brother
Leo, write that this would be perfect joy.

And if constrained by hunger, and the cold,
and the night, we should knock yet again,
and beg him with many tears, for the love
of God, that he would open to us and let us
in, and he should say still more angrily:
' These are importunate rascals, I will pay
them well for this as they deserve,' and
should come out furiously with a knotted
stick, and seize hold of us by our hoods, and
throw us to the earth, and roll us in the snow,
and beat us all over our bodies; if we should
bear all these things patiently and with joy,
thinking on the pains of the blessed Christ,
as that which we ought to bear for His
love, O Brother Leo write, that it is in
this that there is perfect joy. Finally, hear
the conclusion, Brother Leo: above all the
graces and gifts of the Holy Spirit, which
Christ has given to his friends, is that of con-
quering oneself, and suffering willingly for
the love of Christ all pain, ill-usage and opprobrium, and calamity: because of all the
other gifts of God we can glory in none, seeing they are not ours, but God's, as said the
Apostle: What hast thou that thou hast not
received of God ?   And if thou hast received
it of God, why dost thou glory, as if thou
hadst it of thyself?   But in the cross of tribulation and affliction we may glory, for
these are ours ; and therefore, says the Apostle, ' I will not glory save in the cross of our
Lord Jesus Christ.' "

VIII—How St Francis taught Brother Leo
how to answer him, and the Brother
could not say anything but the contrary
of what St Francis desired

ONCE on a time, in the beginning of the
order, St Francis was lodged with Brother
Leo in a place where there were no books to
say the divine office with. And when
the hour came for matins, St Francis said
to Brother Leo : " My beloved, we have no
breviary with which to say matins, but in
order that we may spend the time in praising God, I will speak, and thou shalt
answer as I shall instruct thee, and take
heed that thou say not a word other than as I
tell thee. I will say thus : ' O Brother
Francis, thou hast done so many evils and
so many sins in thy time, that thou hast
merited hell ; ' and thou, Brother Leo, shalt
answer : ' Truly, and thou dost merit the
deepest hell.' " And Brother Leo, with the
simplicity of a little dove, replied : " Willingly, father ; begin, in the name of God."
Then St Francis began to say : " O
Brother Francis, thou hast done so many
evils and so many sins in thy time, that
thou hast merited hell." And Brother Leo
replied : " God will work so much good
through thee, that thou shalt go to paradise." Then said St Francis : " Say not
thus, Brother Leo, but when I shall say :
' Brother Francis, thou hast committed so

many iniquities against God, that thou art
worthy to be accursed of God,' do thou answer thus : 'Verily thou art worthy to be
placed among the accursed.'" And Brother Leo replied : "Willingly, father."

Again St Francis, with many tears and
sighs, beating his breast, said with a loud
voice : "O my Lord, Lord of heaven and
earth, I have committed against Thee so
many iniquities, and so many grievous sins
that I am worthy to be accursed of Thee for
them all ; " and Brother Leo replied : "O
Brother Francis, God will make thee such,
that amongst the blessed thou shalt be singularly blessed." And St Francis, marvelling that Brother Leo answered contrariwise
to what he had imposed on him, reproved
him, saying : "Wherefore dost thou not answer as I instructed thee ? I command thee,
by holy obedience, to answer as I will tell
thee. I will speak thus : 'O Brother Francis, thou wicked little one, dost thou think
that God will have mercy on thee, knowing
that thou hast committed so many sins
against the God of mercy and God of all consolation, that thou art not worthy to find
mercy ?' And thou Brother Leo, little sheep,
shalt answer : 'By no means art thou worthy to find mercy.'"

But when St Francis said : "O Brother
Francis, thou wicked one," and the rest,
Brother Leo answered him : "God the
Father, whose mercy is infinitely more than
thy sins, will show thee great mercy, and,

more than this, will add to thee many graces." At which reply, St Francis, gently angry and patiently wrath, said to Brother Leo: "And wherefore hast thou presumed to act contrary to obedience, and so many times answered the contrary to what I imposed on thee?" Brother Leo replied humbly and reverently: "God knows, my father, that each time I had it in my heart to answer as thou hadst commanded me, but God makes me speak as it pleases Him, and not as it pleases me." At which St Francis marvelled, and said to Brother Leo: "I pray thee from my heart that this time thou wilt answer me as I have told thee." And Brother Leo answered: "I speak in the name of God, for this time I will answer as thou desirest."

And St Francis said, weeping: "O Brother Francis, thou little wicked one, dost thou think God will have mercy on thee?" Brother Leo replied: "Yea, rather, thou shalt receive great grace from God, and He will exalt thee, and glorify thee to all eternity, because he that humbleth; himself shall be exalted, and I cannot say otherwise, for God speaks by my mouth." And in this humble contention, with many tears and much spiritual consolation, they continued till the end of the day.

IX—How Brother Masseo mockingly said to
St Francis that all the world went after
him; and St Francis replied that this
was for the confusion of the world and
for the glory of God

ST FRANCIS was staying once on a time in
the convent of the Portiuncula with Brother
Masseo of Marignano, a man of great sanctity, discernment, and grace in speaking of
the things of God, for which reason St
Francis loved him much. And one day, as
St Francis was returning from his prayers
in the wood, at the entrance to the wood
Brother Masseo met him; and, wishing
to test how humble he was, asked in a
mocking manner, saying: "Why after
thee? why after thee? why after thee?" St
Francis replied : "What is it thou wouldst
say?" And Brother Masseo answered :
"Say, why is it that all the world comes after
thee, and everybody desires to see thee, and
to hear thee, and to obey thee? Thou art
not a man either comely of person, or of
noble birth, or of great science; whence then
comes it that all the world runs after thee?

Hearing this St Francis, filled with joy
in his spirit, raised his face towards heaven,
and remained for a great while with his
mind lifted up to God; then, returning to
himself, he knelt down, and gave praise and
thanks to God; and then, with great fervour of spirit, turning to Brother Masseo,

D

he said : " Wouldst know why after me ?
wouldst know why after me ? why all the
world runs after me ? This comes to me,
because the eyes of the most high God,
which behold in all places both the evil and
the good, even those most holy eyes have
not seen amongst sinners one more vile, nor
more insufficient, nor a greater sinner than I,
and therefore to do that wonderful work
which He intends to do He has not found
on earth a viler creature than I ; and for this
cause has He elected me to confound the no-
bility and the grandeur and the strength
and beauty and wisdom of the world; that
all men may know that all virtue and all
goodness are of Him and not of the creature, and that none should glory in His
presence, but that he who glories should
glory in the Lord to whom is all honour
and glory in eternity." Then Brother
Masseo at this humble and fervent reply
feared within himself, and knew certainly
that St Francis was grounded in humility.

X—How St Francis made Brother Masseo
    turn round and round, and then went
    on to Siena

ST FRANCIS was going along the road one
day with Brother Masseo, and the said Brother Masseo had gone on a little in front ;
and coming to where three ways met, by
which one might go either to Florence, to
Siena or to Arezzo, Brother Masseo said :

" Father, by which of these ways are we to
go?" And St Francis answered: "By which-
ever God wills." Said Brother Masseo:
"And how are we to know the will of God?"
St Francis replied: "By the sign which I
shall show thee; and I command thee, by the
merit of holy obedience, that thou stand on
thy feet in the place where these three ways
meet, and turn round and round as children
do, and cease not to turn unless I tell thee."

Then Brother Masseo began to turn round
and round, and did it so often that, through
giddiness of the head which is caused by
continual turning, he fell several times to
the ground; but as St Francis did not tell
him to stop, willing to obey faithfully he
rose again each time. At last, when he was
turning very rapidly, St Francis said:
" Stand still and do not move." And he did
so. And St Francis asked him: " Which
way is thy face?" Said Brother Masseo:
" Towards Siena." Then said St Francis:
"This is the way God would have us to go."

Now as they went along the way,
Brother Masseo wondered that St Francis
had made him behave as the children do
before the seculars who were passing by;
but out of reverence for the holy father he
did not venture to say anything. And they
having come now to Siena, as soon as the
people of the city heard of the arrival of the
saint they went to meet him and, out of devotion, they carried him and his companion
straight to the bishop's house in such wise

that they did not touch the ground with their feet. At that time all the men of Siena were at strife with each other, and two of them had been killed; but St Francis having come to them, he preached to them with so great devotion and sanctity that he brought them all to peace and to great unity and concord one with another. For this cause the bishop of Siena, hearing of the holy work which St Francis had done, invited him to his house, and received him with great honour both that day and the night following.

And the next morning St Francis, the truly humble who in all his works sought nothing but the glory of God, rose early with his companion, and departed without taking leave of the bishop. For which cause Brother Masseo murmured within himself as he went along the way, saying: "What is this that this good man has done? He made me act as a child, and to the bishop who did him so much honour he said not so much as a word, nor returned him thanks;" and it seemed to Brother Masseo that St Francis had behaved himself indiscreetly in this. But having by the divine inspiration returned to himself, he reproved himself in his heart, and said: "Thou art too proud who dost judge the work of God, and art worthy of hell for thy indiscreet pride; for indeed Brother Francis did yesterday so holy a work that, if an angel of God had done it, it had not been more marvellous; therefore if he bade thee throw stones thou oughtest to do so and to obey; for what he

did on this road came from the divine inspiration, as was shown by the good ending that
followed it; because, had he not pacified
these fierce people who strove with each
other, not only would many more of them
have suffered the death of the body, as had
already begun to be the case, but many souls
would have been dragged to hell by the
devil; and therefore art thou most foolish and
proud who murmurest at what manifestly
proceeds from the will of God."

And all this, which Brother Masseo said
within his own heart going on in front, was
revealed by God to St Francis; and
presently, approaching him St Francis
said : " Those things which thou thinkest
now hold fast, for they are good and useful
and inspired by God; but thy first murmuring was blind and proud and vain and was
put into thy heart by the devil." Then
Brother Masseo saw clearly that St Francis
knew the secrets of his heart, and understood
certainly that the holy father was directed
by the Divine Wisdom in all that he did.

XI—How St Francis imposed on Brother
Masseo the office of the door and of the
kitchen and of the almsgiving; and afterwards at the prayers of the others re-
leased him

ST FRANCIS desired to humble Brother
Masseo, in order that the many graces which
God had given him might not lift him up

with vainglory, but that, by virtue of his humility, he might grow in them from virtue to virtue. And as he was dwelling in a solitary place with his first companions, men of true sanctity of whom Brother Masseo was one, he said one day to the said Brother Masseo before all the company: "See, Brother Masseo, all these thy companions have the gifts of contemplation and of prayer, but thou hast the gift of preaching the word of God and of satisfying the people: and therefore I will, in order that these others may give themselves to contemplation, that thou shouldst perform the office of the door and of the kitchen and of the almsgiving; and that, when the other brothers eat, thou shouldst eat beside the door of the house; so that whoever comes to the house, when they knock thou shouldst satisfy them with some good words from God, so that none of them need go to any but thee; and this do by the merit of holy obedience."

Then Brother Masseo drew on his hood, and bowed his head, and humbly received and continued in this obedience, by which he fulfilled the office of the door and of the kitchen and of the almsgiving. At which his companions, being men illuminated of God, began to feel great reproach in their hearts, considering that Brother Masseo was a man of as great or even of greater perfection than they, and that on him was laid all the burden of the house, and not on them. Therefore they were all of one mind, and went together to the holy father to pray

that it would please him to divide amongst
them these offices, inasmuch as their conscience could by no means endure it that
Brother Masseo should bear so many
labours. Hearing this St Francis yielded
to their counsel and consented to their will;
and having called Brother Masseo, he said
to him: "Brother Masseo, thy companions
desire to share the offices that I gave to thee,
and therefore I desire that these offices should
be divided." And Brother Masseo, with
great humility and patience, said: "Father,
that which thou appointest me, whether the
whole or a part I account it all as from God."

Then St Francis, seeing the charity of
the others and the humility of Brother
Masseo, preached to them a marvellous discourse on holy humility, showing that the
greater the gifts and the graces of God the
more humble we ought to be, since without
humility no virtue is acceptable to God.
And having delivered his discourse, he distributed the offices amongst them with the
greatest affection.

❦

XII—How St Francis and Brother Masseo
    placed some bread which they had begged
    on a stone beside a fountain; and St
    Francis greatly praised Poverty; and how
    St Peter and St Paul appeared to him

THE wonderful servant and follower of
Christ, St Francis, in order to conform
himself perfectly in all things to Christ—

who, as it is said in the Gospel, sent out His
disciples, two and two, to all the cities and
places whither He was intending to go—
had, after the example of Christ, chosen
twelve companions, and sent them forth into
the world to preach, two and two. And in
order to give them an example of true
obedience, he was the first to set forth, after
the example of Christ, who began to act
before He taught. Now, having assigned
to the others another part of the world, he
himself, with Brother Masseo for companion,
took the way which leads towards the land
of France.

And coming one day to a certain town
and being very hungry, they went, according to the rule, to beg bread for the love of
God; St Francis going down one street and
Brother Masseo down another. But, because St Francis was a man of mean
appearance and small of stature and accounted a vile beggar by those who knew
him not, he received nothing but a few
mouthfuls and crumbs of dry bread; whilst
Brother Masseo, being tall and comely in
person, had good pieces and large and
many given to him, and entire loaves.
When they had begged enough, they went
together to a place outside the town, where
there was a fair fountain, that they might
eat; and beside which was also a broad
and convenient stone, on which each placed
all the alms which he had begged.

And St Francis, seeing that the pieces

of bread which Brother Masseo had were
larger and better than his own, had great
joy, and spoke thus: "O Brother Masseo,
we are not worthy of so great treasure."
And as he repeated these words several
times, Brother Masseo answered him:
"Father, how can this be called treasure,
when we are in such poverty, and lack the
things of which we have need; we, who
have neither cloth, nor knives, nor plates,
nor porringer, nor house, nor table, nor man-
servant, nor maidservant?" Then said St
Francis: "And this is what I call a great
treasure, that there is nothing here provided
by human industry, but everything is provided by Divine Providence, as we may see
manifestly in this bread which we have
begged, in this stone which serves so beautifully for our table, and in this so clear
fountain; and therefore I desire that we
should pray to God, that He would cause
holy poverty, which is a thing so noble that
God himself was made subject to it, to be
loved by us with our whole heart."

And when he had said these words, and
they had made their prayer, and partaken
for bodily refreshment of the pieces of bread,
and drunk of the water, they arose, and
went on their way to France. And they
having come to a church, St Francis said
to his companion: "Let us go into this
church and pray." And entering, St Francis placed himself behind the altar, and
betook himself to prayer. And as he prayed,

he received from the divine visitation such excessive fervour, which so vehemently inflamed his soul with the love of holy poverty, that by the increased colour of his face, and the unaccustomed opening of his lips, it seemed as though he were breathing out flames of love. And coming thus, all inflamed, to his companion, he said to him: "Ah! ah! ah! Brother Masseo, yield thyself to me." And this he said three times, and the third time, he lifted Brother Masseo by his breath into the air, and threw him from him, to the distance of a long spear, which put Brother Masseo into the greatest astonishment. And afterwards, relating the matter to his companions he said that, during the time he was raised up and thrown forth by the breath which proceeded from St Francis, he tasted such sweetness in his soul and such consolation of the Holy Spirit, that in all his life he had never felt the like.

And this done, St Francis said to him: "My brother, let us go to St Peter and St Paul, and pray them to teach us and to give us to possess the immeasurable treasure of holy poverty, inasmuch as it is a treasure so exalted and so divine that we are not worthy to possess it in our vile bodies, seeing that this is that celestial virtue by which all earthly and transitory things are trodden under foot and all impediments are lifted away from the soul, so that she can freely unite herself to the eternal God. And this is the virtue which makes the soul, while still retained on earth, converse with the angels in heaven, and this it is which accompanied Christ to His cross, with Christ was buried, with Christ was raised up, with Christ ascended into heaven ; which, being given in this life to the souls who are enamoured of it, facilitates their flight to heaven, seeing that it guards the arms of true humility and charity. And therefore let us pray the most holy apostles of Christ, who were perfect lovers of this pearl of the Gospel of Christ, that they will beg for us this grace from our Lord Jesus Christ, that by His most holy mercy He would grant us the merit to be true lovers, observers, and humble disciples of this most precious, most lovable, evangelical poverty."

And thus speaking, they arrived in Rome, and entered the church of St Peter ; and St Francis placed himself in prayer in a corner of the church, and Brother Masseo in another. And as St Francis prayed for a long time with many tears and great devotion, the most holy apostles Peter and Paul appeared to him in great splendour, and said : " Because thou has asked and desired to observe that which Christ and the holy apostles observed, the Lord Jesus Christ has sent us to thee to announce that thy prayer is heard, and it is granted of God to thee and thy followers to possess perfectly the treasure of most holy poverty And further, in His name, we say to thee that whosoever, after thy example, shall fol-

low perfectly after this desire, he shall be
secure of the blessedness of life eternal ; and
thou and all thy followers shall be blessed of
God." And having said these words they
vanished, leaving St Francis full of consolation, who, rising from his prayer, returned
to his companion, and asked him if God had
revealed nothing to him ; and he answered
him, " Nothing." Then St Francis told him
how the holy apostles had appeared to him,
and what they had revealed to him. At
which both of them, filled with joy, determined to return by the valley of Spoleto,
and to abandon the journey into France.

XIII—As St Francis and his Brothers were speaking of our Divine Lord, He appeared in their midst

ST FRANCIS, in the beginning of his religious life having retired with his companions
to speak together of Christ, in the fervour
of his spirit he commanded one of them, in
the name of God, to open his mouth, and to
speak of God as the Holy Spirit should inspire him. As soon as the brother fulfilled
the command, and spoke of God marvellously, St Francis imposed silence on him,
and gave the same command to another brother. This one also obeyed, and spoke of
God with subtle insight, and St Francis imposed silence on him also, and commanded
a third to speak of God ; and he similarly began to speak so profoundly of the secret

things of God, that St Francis knew certainly that, like the other two, he spoke by inspiration of the Holy Spirit. And this was proved also by example and by express sign ; for, as they were thus speaking, there appeared the blessed Christ in the midst of them, under the appearance and form of a beautiful youth, and blessed them all, filling them all with so much grace and sweetness, that they were all ravished out of themselves and lay as though dead not feeling anything of this world. And then, returning to himself, St Francis said to them : " My beloved brothers, render thanks to God, who has willed, by the mouth of the simple, to reveal the treasures of the Divine Wisdom ; because God is He who opens the mouth of the dumb, and makes the tongue of the simple to speak most wisely."

XIV—How St Clare ate with St Francis and his companion Brothers at St Mary of the Angels

WHEN St Francis was staying at Assisi, he went several times to visit St Clare, and to give her holy instructions. She had a very great desire to eat with him for once, and prayed him for this many times; but he would not consent to give her this consolation. When his companions had heard of the desire of St Clare, they said to St Francis : " Father, this stiffness seems to us not according to divine charity, seeing

Sister Clare is a virgin, which is a thing holy and well-pleasing to God—namely, that thou shouldst refuse her in such a little matter as eating with thee; and especially considering that at thy preaching she abandoned the riches and pomps of the world. And to say the truth, if she asked thee a greater favour than this, thou oughtest to do it for this thy spiritual plant." Then St Francis answered : " Does it seem to you that I ought to consent ? " and his companions replied : " Father, yes ; a right thing it is that thou shouldst grant her this favour and consolation." Then said St Francis : " Since it seems so to you, it seems so to me also ; but, that she may be more consoled, I will have her eat with me at St Mary of the Angels, because she has been so long a time secluded at St Damian's, that it will give her joy to see the place of the Blessed Mary, where she was shorn and made the spouse of Jesus Christ; and there we shall eat together in the name of God."

The day appointed therefore having come, St Clare, with one companion, came out of her convent and, accompanied by the companions of St Francis, went to St Mary of the Angels, and saluted devoutly before her altar the holy Virgin Mary, in the place where her hair had been cut off and where she had received the veil. Then they led her into the house, until it should be the hour to dine. And meanwhile St Francis had the dinner-table prepared on the bare ground, as was his custom. And the hour for dinner being come, they seated themselves together, St Francis and St Clare, and one of the companions of St Francis with the companion of St Clare, and then all the other companions humbly seating themselves round the table. And at the first dish St Francis began to talk of God in a manner so sweet, so admirable, and so sublime that there descended upon them the abundance of divine grace, and they were all ravished in God.

And as they were thus ravished with their eyes and their hands raised towards heaven, the men of Assisi and of Bettona and of the surrounding country saw that St Mary of the Angels and the whole house, and the wood which led up to the house were burning brightly ; and it seemed as though a great fire filled the church and the house and the whole wood together, so that they ran thither with great haste to extinguish the flames, verily believing that the whole place was on fire. But when they came to the house and found nothing, they entered and found St Francis and St Clare, with all their company, sitting round this humble table, and ravished in the comtemplation of God. From this they understood with certainty that what they had seen was a divine and not a material fire, which God had caused miraculously to appear, in order to show and to signify the fire of divine love which inflamed the souls of these holy brothers and holy religious; and they departed with great consolation in their hearts and holy edification.

Then after a long space St Francis returned to himself, and St Clare also with all the others, and felt well comforted within themselves by their spiritual nourishment, little as they had partaken of the bodily refreshment. And afterwards, this blessed feast being ended, St Clare, well escorted, returned to St Damian's; where the sisters seeing her had great joy, for they feared lest St Francis had sent her to govern some other convent, just as he had sent Sister Agnes, their holy sister, as abbess to govern the convent of Monticelli at Florence; and since St Francis had said one time to St Clare : " Be ready, in case I have need to send thee to another house ;" and she, as the daughter of holy obedience, had answered : " Father, I am ready always to go wheresoever thou wilt send me." And therefore the sisters rejoiced greatly when they saw her again; and St Clare received from this also much consolation.

XV—How St Francis received the council of St Clare and of the holy Brother Silvester, that he should preach for the conversion of many; and how he founded the Third Order, and preached to the birds

THE humble servant of Christ, St Francis, a short time after his conversion, having already gathered many companions and re-

ceived them into the order, entered into
great consideration and great doubt what
he should do : whether he should give himself solely to prayer, or whether he should
sometimes preach ; and he desired much
to know the will of God in this matter.
And, because the holy humility that was
in him suffered him not to presume on
himself nor on his own prayers, he thought
to discover the divine will through the
prayers of others. And he called Brother
Masseo, and spoke thus : "Go to Sister
Clare and tell her from me to pray fervently
to God, she and some of her most spiritual
daughters, that it may please Him to show
which is the best, whether I should give
myself to preaching or solely to prayer;
and then go to Brother Silvester and say
the same to him." The same Brother
Silvester it was who, when he was in the
secular state, had seen a cross of gold proceeding from the mouth of St Francis,
which went lengthwise as far as heaven
and the arms of which extended to the
extremities of the world ; and the same
Brother Silvester was also of so great
devotion and sanctity that many times he
spoke with God, and whatsoever he asked
of God was granted, and for this cause St
Francis had a great devotion towards him.

Brother Masseo therefore departed, and,
according to the command of St Francis,
made his embassy first to St Clare, and
afterwards to Brother Silvester who, as

E

soon as he knew wherefore he had come,
immediately betook himself to prayer.
And when he had received the divine
answer, he turned to Brother Masseo and
spoke thus : " This is what God says : thou
shalt tell Brother Francis that God has not
called him to this state solely for himself,
but that he may gain much fruit in the
souls of others, and that many through him
may be saved."

Having received this answer, Brother
Masseo returned to St Clare to know what
she had obtained of God ; and she replied
that she and her companions had received
from God the same answer as Brother
Silvester. With this reply Brother Masseo
returned to St Francis ; and St Francis
received him with the greatest charity,
washed his feet, and prepared his repast.
And after he had eaten St Francis called
him into the wood, and kneeling before
him, he let down his hood, and stretching
out his arms in the form of the cross, he
asked : " What does my Lord Jesus Christ
command that I should do ? " Brother
Masseo answered : " As to Brother Silvester,
so to Sister Clare with her sisters, has
Christ answered and revealed that His will
is that thou shouldst go into the world to
preach, because He has not elected thee for
thyself alone, but also for the salvation
of others." Then St Francis, having heard
this reply and knowing by this what was
the will of Jesus Christ, arose with great

fervour and said : " Let us go in the name
of God ; " and he took for his companions
Brother Masseo and Brother Agnolo, both
holy men.

And going by the prompting of the
Holy Ghost, without taking thought of
the way or the road, he came to a village
Savurniano. And St Francis began to
preach : and first of all he commanded the
swallows who were singing that they should
keep silence until he had done preaching,
and the swallows obeyed him. And he
preached with so much fervour that all
the men and women in that village were
minded to go forth and abandon the village.
But St Francis suffered them not, and said
to them : " Do not be in haste, and do not
go hence, and I will order that which you
must do for the salvation of your souls ; "
and then he thought of his third order
for the salvation of the whole world. And
he left them much comforted and well
disposed to penance ; and he departed
thence, and went by Cannaio and Bevagno.

And passing along, in fervour of soul, he
lifted up his eyes and saw many trees standing by the way, and filled with a countless
multitude of little birds ; at which St Francis
wondered, and said to his companions :
" Wait a little for me in the road, and I will
go and preach to my sisters the birds."
And he entered into the field, and began to
preach to the birds that were on the ground.
And suddenly, those that were in the trees

came around him, and together they all remained silent, so long as it pleased St Francis to speak; and even after he had finished
they would not depart until he had given
them his blessing. And according as Brother Masseo afterwards related to Brother
James of La Massa, St Francis went among
them and touched them with his cloak, and
none of them moved.

The substance of the sermon was this:
" My little sisters, the birds, you are much
beholden to God your creator, and in all
places you ought to praise Him, because He
has given you liberty to fly about in all
places, and has given you double and triple
raiment. Know also, that He preserved
your race in the ark of Noe that your spe-
cies might not perish. And again, you are
beholden to Him for the element of air,
which he has appointed for you; and for this
also, that you neither sow nor reap, but God
feeds you and gives you the brooks and
fountains for your drink, the mountains and
valleys also for your refuge, and the tall
trees wherein to make your nests. And
since you know neither how to sew nor to
spin, God clothes you, you and your young
ones. Wherefore your creator loves you
much, since he has bestowed on you so many
benefits. And therefore beware, my little
sisters, of the sin of ingratitude, and study
always to please God."

As St Francis spoke thus to them, all
the multitude of these birds opened their

beaks, and stretched out their necks, and
opened their wings ; and reverently bowing
their heads to the earth, by their acts and by
their songs they showed that the words of the
holy father gave them the greatest delight.
And St Francis rejoiced, and was glad with
them, and marvelled much at such a multitude of birds, and at their beautiful variety,
and their attention and familiarity ; for all
which he devoutly praised their Creator in
them. Finally, having finished his sermon,
St Francis made the sign of the cross over
them, and gave them leave to depart ; and
thereupon all those birds arose in the air,
with wonderful singing ; and after the fashion
of the sign of the cross which St Francis
had made over them, they divided themselves into four parts ; and one part flew
towards the east, and another to the west,
another to the south, and another to the
north ; and all departing went their way
singing wonderful songs, signifying by this
that as St Francis, standard-bearer of the
cross of Christ, had preached to them and
made on them the sign of the cross, after
which they had divided themselves, going to
the four parts of the world, so the preaching of the cross of Christ, renewed by St
Francis, should be carried by him and by
his brothers to the whole world, and that
these brothers, after the fashion of the birds,
should possess nothing of their own in this
world, but commit their lives solely to the
providence of God.

XVI—How a little boy-brother, whilst St
Francis was praying in the night, saw
Christ and the Virgin Mother and many
other Saints talking to him

A CERTAIN little boy, most pure and innocent, was received into the order during the
lifetime of St Francis, and it was in a little
place where the brothers, of necessity, slept
on truckle beds. Now once on a time, St
Francis came to this place, and in the evening, after compline, he lay down to sleep,
that he might be able to rise in the night
and pray when the other brothers were
asleep, according to his custom. Then the
little boy set his heart on carefully watching
the ways of St Francis, that he might know
his sanctity, and especially that he might
know what he did when he got up in the
night. And in order that he might not
sleep too soundly, the boy, when he lay
down by the side of St Francis tied his cord
to the cord of St Francis, that he might feel
when he got up; and of this St Francis perceived nothing.

But in the night, after his first sleep, when
all the other brothers slept, St Francis arose
and found his cord fastened to something,
and he softly untied it, so that the boy did
not feel anything, and went into the wood
which was close to the house, and entering
a little cell which was there, betook himself
to prayer. After a while the boy awoke, and

finding that the cord had been unfastened and that St Francis had arisen and gone away, he arose also, and went to look for him : and finding the door open which led to the wood, he thought that St Francis might have gone there, and entered the wood himself.

And nearing the cell where St Francis was praying, he began to hear much speaking; and approaching nearer to see, and to make out what it was that he heard, he beheld a wonderful light which surrounded St Francis ; and in it he saw Christ, and the Blessed Virgin Mary, and St John the Baptist, and St John the Evangelist, and an immense multitude of angels, who were speaking with St Francis. Seeing and hearing all this, the boy fell to the earth as one dead. Then, the mysterious vision being ended, St Francis, returning to the house, stumbled with his foot against the boy who lay as though dead ; and in compassion, he lifted him up and carried him in his arms, as a good shepherd does with his lambs. And afterwards learning from the boy how he had seen this vision, he commanded him not to tell it to anyone as long as he should be alive. And the boy grew in great grace with God and devotion to St Francis, and became a celebrated man in the order; and after the death of St Francis he revealed to the brothers the vision which he had seen,

XVII—Of the marvellous Chapter which St Francis held at St Mary of the Angels, at which were present more than five thousand Brothers

THE faithful servant of Christ, Francis, was once holding a general chapter at St Mary of the Angels, at which chapter more than five thousand brothers assembled; and there came also St Dominic, head and founder of the order of Friars Preachers, who was then on his way from Borgogna to Rome. And hearing of the assembling of the chapter, which St Francis was holding in the plain of St Mary of the Angels, he went to see it, with seven brothers of his order. There was also at the said chapter a cardinal most devoted to St Francis, who had prophesied to him that he should be pope, as it afterwards came to pass. This cardinal had come expressly from Perugia, where the court was, to Assisi; and he came every day to see St Francis and his brothers, and sometimes sang the Mass, and sometimes preached to the brothers in chapter. The said cardinal found the greatest delight and devotion whenever he came to visit the holy company.

And coming to the little plain of St Mary of the Angels, he saw the brothers grouped in companies : here forty, there a hundred, there eighty together, all occupied in speaking of the things of God, in prayer, in tears,

and in exercises of charity; and this with
such quietness, and such modesty, that there
was not heard one sound, or any disturbance.
And marvelling at such a multitude, so well
ordered, he said, with tears and great devotion: "Truly this is the camp and the army
of the knights of God." There was not to
be heard in all this multitude an idle word
or unseemly jest; but wherever a company
of brothers assembled together, they either
prayed, or said the office, or wept over their
own sins and those of their benefactors, or
spoke of the things which are for the salvation of souls. The tents in this encampment
were of willow-trellis and of rush matting,
and divided into groups consisting of the
brothers of the various provinces; and hence
this chapter was called "the Chapter of the
trellises," or, "of the rush-mats." Their
bed was on the bare ground, with a little
straw for those who had it; and for pillows
they had stones or logs of wood. For
which cause, so great devotion spread from
them to those who heard or saw them, and
so great was the fame of their sanctity, that
from the court of the pope, which was then
at Perugia, and from the other districts of
the valley of Spoleto, there came many
counts, barons, and cavaliers, and other gentlemen of rank, and many parish priests,
cardinals, bishops and abbots, and many
other clerics, to see this so great and holy and
humble congregation, like which the world
had never another containing so many holy

men together. And chiefly they came to
see the most holy head and father of this
holy people, who had robbed from the
world so noble a prey, and assembled together so devout and fair a flock to follow
in the steps of the true shepherd Jesus Christ.

The general chapter being therefore assembled, the holy father and general minister of all, St Francis, with fervour of spirit,
expounded the word of God : and preached
to them with a loud voice that which the
Holy Spirit made him speak; and for the
theme of his sermon, he proposed to them
these words : " My sons, great are the things
promised to us from God : yea, too, great
things are promised to us, if we observe that
which we have promised to Him. Brief are
the delights of this world; the pain which
follows after them is perpetual : little are the
pains of this life ; but the glory of the other
life is infinite." And on these words he
preached with the greatest devotion, comforting the brothers, and persuading them
to obey and reverence the holy mother
Church, and to have fraternal charity, to
praise God for all men, and to have patience
in the adversities of this world, and temperance in prosperity, and to observe modesty
and angelic chastity, and to have peace and
concord with God and with men, and with
their own conscience, and to love and observe holy poverty. And after this, he said :
"I command all you who are here assembled,
by virtue of obedience, that none of you have

care or solicitude for anything to eat, or anything necessary for the body; attend only to
praying and praising God, and all solicitude
for your body leave to Him, inasmuch as He
has special care for you." And all received
this command with glad hearts and with joyful countenances; and the sermon of St
Francis being ended, they prostrated themselves in prayer. At which St Dominic, who
was present during all these things, marvelled greatly at the commandment of St Francis, and considered it indiscreet, not being
able to think how so great a multitude should
be able to govern itself, without any care or
solicitude for the things necessary to the
body.

But the chief shepherd, Christ the
blessed, willing to show how He has care
for His sheep, and singular love for His poor,
immediately inspired the people of Perugia,
of Spoleto, of Foligno, of Spello, and Assisi,
and the other surrounding districts, so that
they carried what was needed to eat and to
drink to this holy congregation. And behold there came speedily, from the neigh-
bouring districts, men with mules, horses
and carts, laden with bread and with wine,
with beans, and with cheese, and with other
good things to eat, such as the poor of Christ
had need of. Besides this, they brought nap-
kins, earthen pots, bowls, drinking cups, and
other vessels necessary for so great a multitude; and he considered himself blessed
who could bring the most, or serve the most

diligently; so that even the knights and barons, and other gentlemen, who had come to see the sight, were the first, with great humility and devotion, to serve them.

For which cause, St Dominic, seeing these things, and knowing of a surety that Divine Providence worked for them, humbly acknowledged that he had wrongfully judged that St Francis had given an indiscreet commandment, and forthwith went, and kneeling down, humbly confessed his fault; and added: "Truly God has special care of these holy poor little ones, and I knew it not; and from this hour, I promise, first of all, to observe holy, evangelical poverty; and I anathematize, on the part of God, all the brothers of my order who shall presume to have poverty." Thus was St Dominic much edified by the faith of most holy Francis, and the obedience and poverty of so great and well-ordered a company, and by the providence of God and the copious abundance of all these good things.

In the same chapter St Francis was told that many brothers wore leather bands with sharp points piercing their flesh, and sharp-pointed chains of iron, from which cause many were infirm, and some were dying, and many were impeded in prayer. Whereupon St Francis, as a wise father, commanded, by holy obedience, that those who had such leather bands or sharp-pointed chains should take them off, and put them down before him; and this was done; and there were counted

more than five hundred iron chains with
sharp points, and many more circlets, either
for the arm or the loins, so that they made
a great heap; and St Francis made them be
left there. After which the chapter was
concluded ; and St Francis, comforting them
all in that which is good, and exhorting them
as to how they should preserve themselves
from sin in this evil world, with the blessing
of God, and his own, dismissed them to their
various provinces all consoled with spiritual
delights.

XVIII—How the Vineyard of the Priest of
Rieti, in whose house St Francis rested,
was despoiled of its grapes, and afterwards
miraculously yielded more wine than here-
tofore ; and how God revealed to St Francis
that he should have Paradise for his portion.

IT happened once that St Francis was suffering from a grievous malady of the eyes,
and the Cardinal Ugolino, protector of the
order, through the great tenderness which he
had for him, wrote to him to come to Rieti
where were the best physicians for the eyes.
Then St Francis, having received the cardinal's letter, set out, going first to St
Damian's, where was St Clare, that most
devoted spouse of Christ, that he might give
her some consolation and thence go on to
the cardinal. Having arrived there the following night, his eyes grew so much worse
that he could not see the light at all ; where-

fore, as he could not go on, St Clare made
for him a little cell of reeds wherein he
might rest commodiously. But St Francis,
what with the pain of his malady, and the
multitude of rats in that place which caused
him the greatest discomfort, could get no
rest either by day or by night. And having
yet more of these pains and sufferings to
sustain, he began to think, and to recognize
that this was a chastisement from God for his
sins; and he began to return thanks to God
with all his heart and with his mouth, and
then wept aloud, and said: "My Lord, I
deserve this and much more, my Lord Jesus
Christ, Good Shepherd, who dost extend
Thy mercy to us sinners through divers
pains and agonies of the body, give grace
and virtue to me, Thy little sheep, that by
no infirmity nor agony nor sorrow may I be
parted from Thee."

And whilst he prayed thus there came to
him a voice from heaven, which said:
"Francis, answer me: if all the earth were
gold, and all seas and streams and fountains
were balsam, and all mountains, hills and
rocks were made of precious stones; and
thou shouldst find another treasure more
noble than these things, even as much as
gold is more noble than earth, balsam than
water and precious stones than mountains
and rocks; and this noble treasure were
given thee through this thine infirmity,
shouldst thou not be truly glad and well
content?" And St Francis answered: "Lord,
I am unworthy of such precious treasures."

And the voice of God said to him: "Rejoice,
Francis, because this is the treasure of life
eternal which I reserve for thee until the
hour when I shall give thee possession of it:
and this infirmity and affliction is the earnest
of that blessed treasure." Then St Francis,
with the greatest joy at so glorious a promise, called his companion, and said: "Let
us go to the cardinal;" and first of all con-
soling St Clare with holy words, and taking
humble leave of her, he took the road towards
Rieti.

And when he was now near the city, such
a multitude of people came forth to meet
him that because of them he would not
enter into it, but turned aside into a church
which was near to the city, about two miles
off. The citizens, knowing that he was in the
said church, ran together so much to see
him that the vineyard of the church was
entirely spoiled, and all the grapes were
plucked; at which the priest grieved much
in his heart, and repented of having received St Francis into his church. But
the thought of the priest being revealed to
St Francis by God, he sent to ask him to
come to him, and said: " Most beloved
father, how many measures of wine did this
vineyard yield thee the year it yielded the
best ?" And he answered: "Twelve measures." Then said St Francis: "I pray thee,
father, to endure patiently my sojourn here
for a few days, because I find here much repose; and let who will pluck the grapes of
thy vineyard for the love of God and of me,

His poor little one; and I promise thee, on
the part of my Lord Jesus Christ, that it
shall yield thee every year twenty measures."
And such use did St Francis make of his
stay there, by the great fruit of souls which
was seen to be gathered from the people
who came to him, that many went away inebriated with the divine love, and abandoned
the world.

The priest confided in the promise of St
Francis, and liberally gave up the vineyard
to all who came to him. And a marvellous
thing! the vineyard was altogether stripped
and plucked so that scarcely were there a
few clusters of grapes to be found in it.
The time of the vintage came; and the priest
gathered such clusters as were left, and put
them in the wine-press, and trod them, and,
according to the promise of St Francis, obtained twenty measures of the best wine.
This miraculous manifestation was intended
to show that as by the merits of St Francis
the vineyard, despoiled of grapes, abounded
in wine; so that the Christian people, barren
of virtue through their sins, by the merits and
doctrine of St Francis should continually
abound with the good fruits of penitence.

XIX—Of a wondrous beautiful Vision seen by
a young Brother.

A CERTAIN young man, who was of noble
birth and very delicate, came into the order
of St Francis; and from the day he entered

it, by the instigation of the devil he began
to have the habit which he wore in such
abomination that he seemed to himself to
be wearing a vile sack. He had a horror of
the sleeves, he abominated the hood, and the
length and roughness of the habit appeared
to him an insupportable burden. And growing still more disgusted with the religious
life, he at last began to entertain the thought
of leaving off the habit and returning to the
world.

He had acquired the custom of passing,
as his master had instructed him, once in
every hour before the altar of the convent
where was deposited the body of Christ,
and there, genuflecting with great reverence,
bowing himself with his hood drawn down,
and his arms crossed. And it came to pass
that the night in which he was going to depart and leave the order, he had occasion
to pass in front of this altar of the convent,
and in passing he genuflected according to
custom, and did reverence. And suddenly
he was ravished in spirit, and was shown
marvellous things from God; for he saw before him an innumerable multitude of saints
going after the manner of a procession, two
and two, clothed in the most beautiful and
precious garments of fine broidery; and their
faces and their hands were resplendent as
the sun, and as they went they were accompanied by hymns and songs of the angels.
Amongst these saints were two more nobly
attired and ornamented than any of the

F

others, and they went surrounded by such a brightness that whosoever beheld them was overcome with great amazement. And at the end of the procession he saw yet another, adorned with such glory that he appeared as though he were a new-made knight more honoured than all the rest. The youth, seeing this, marvelled, and knew not what this procession might mean, nor had he the courage to ask, but remained rapt in ecstacy by the sweetness of the vision.

And the procession having passed by, he at last took courage and ran after those who were last in it, and with great fear asked them, saying: "O beloved ones, I pray you may it please you to tell me what are these marvellous things that I see, and this so august procession?" And they answered him: "Know, little son, that we are all of us Friars Minor come from the glory of paradise." And he asked them again: "Who are those two who shine more resplendently than the others?" And they answered: "Those are St Francis and St Antony: and that last one, whom thou seest so much honoured, is a holy brother who died lately, whom, because he valiantly resisted temptation and persevered to the end, we are leading to the glory of paradise; and these garments, so beautifully embroidered as thou seest, which we wear, were given to us by God in exchange for the rough habit which we patiently wore in religion; and the glorious brightness which

thou seest in us is given us from God for the
humility and patience, and for the holy
poverty, obedience and chastity in which we
served Him unto the end. And therefore,
little son, let not the wearing of the sackcloth of religion, which is so greatly
rewarded, seem hard to thee; for if by the
wearing of this sackcloth of St Francis,
through the love of Christ, thou despise the
world, mortify the flesh and combat valiantly
against the devil, thou shalt have a vesture
like to ours, and the same light of glory."

And these words said, the youth returned
to himself, and much comforted by the vision
he cast from him all temptation, and acknowledged his fault before the guardian and the
brothers; and from that day forth he rather
wished for the roughness of penance and
coarse clothing; and finished his life in the
order in great sanctity.

XX—Of the miracle which St Francis performed when he converted the Wolf of Gubbio

AT the time when St Francis dwelt in the
city of Gubbio there appeared in the neighbourhood an enormous wolf, terrible and
ferocious, which devoured not only animals
but even men also, insomuch that all the
citizens stood in great terror because many
times he had approached the city. And all
carried arms when they went out of the city
as though they were going to battle; yet
with all this if anyone met him alone he could

not defend himself against him. And for fear of this wolf it had come to such a pass that no one had the courage to go out of the city. Therefore St Francis had compassion on the men of the place, and desired to go out to this wolf, although all the citizens together counselled him not to do so: and making the sign of the most holy cross he went out into the fields, he and his companions, all his confidence resting in God. And the others hesitating to go any further, St Francis took his way to the place where the wolf was.

And behold! seeing the many citizens who had come out to witness the miracle, the wolf made at St Francis with open mouth. And when he had come near, St Francis made on him the sign of the most holy cross, and called him to him, saying: "Come along, Brother Wolf, I command thee on the part of Christ, that thou do no harm, neither to me nor to anyone." And O wonder! immediately St Francis had made the holy sign the terrible wolf shut his mouth, and ceased to run, and did as he was commanded, coming gently as a lamb, and lay down to rest at the feet of St Francis. Then St Francis spoke to him thus: "Brother Wolf, thou hast done much damage in these parts, and many evil deeds, ravaging and killing the creatures of God, without His permission ; and not only killing and devouring the cattle, but having the hardihood to destroy men made in the image of God ; for

which cause thou dost deserve to be hung
upon the gallows like a convict, as being a
thief and the worst of murderers; and all
the people cry out and murmur because of
thee, and the whole neighbourhood is hostile
to thee. But, Brother Wolf, I would make
peace between them and thee, so that thou
offend no more, and they shall pardon thee
all past offences, and neither men nor dogs
shall persecute thee more."

At these words, the wolf, by the motions
of his body and his tail and his eyes and by
inclining his head, showed that he accepted
what St Francis had said, and was ready to
observe it. Then St Francis said again:
"Brother Wolf, since it pleases thee to
make and to keep this peace, I promise thee
that I shall have thy food given to thee continually by the men of this place as long as
thou shalt live, so that thou shalt suffer no
more hunger, for I know well that it is
hunger which made thee do all this evil.
But since I have obtained for thee this grace,
I desire, Brother Wolf, that thou promise
me never more to harm man or beast; dost
thou promise me this?" And the wolf by
inclining his head made evident signs that
he promised. And St Francis said to him:
"Brother Wolf, I would have thee pledge
me thy faith that thou wilt keep this
promise, without which I cannot well trust
thee." And St Francis, holding out his
hand to receive his faith, the wolf immediately lifted up his right paw and gently

placed it in the hand of St Francis, thus giving him such pledge of faith as he was able.

Then St Francis said: " Brother Wolf, I command thee in the name of Jesus Christ that thou come now with me, without doubting of anything; and let us go and confirm this peace in the name of God." And the wolf obediently went with him like a mild and gentle lamb; which the citizens saw, and marvelled greatly.

And immediately the news spread over the whole city, and all the people, men and women, great and small, young and old, thronged to the piazza to see the wolf with St Francis. And all the people being gathered together, St Francis got up to preach, telling them amongst other things how it was on account of sin that God permitted such calamities, and also pestilences. "Much more terrible," he said, " are the flames of hell which the damned will have to endure eternally, than the fangs of the wolf which cannot destroy more than the body. How much more then are the jaws of hell to be feared, when we see so many held in terror by the jaws of a little animal ! Turn therefore, beloved, to God, and do worthy penance for your sins, and God will deliver you now from the fires of hell."

And the sermon ended, St Francis said: " Listen, my brethren: Brother Wolf, who is here before you, has promised, and has pledged me his faith to make peace with

you, and never to offend again in anything;
and you will promise to give him every day
that which is necessary ; and I make myself
surety for him, that he will faithfully observe
the treaty of peace." Then all the people
promised with one voice to feed him continually. And St Francis, before them all
said to the wolf : "And thou, Brother Wolf,
dost thou promise to observe and to keep
the treaty of peace that thou wilt not offend
either man or beast, or any creature ?" And
the wolf knelt down and inclined his head,
and by gentle movements of his body and
his tail and his ears, showed as well as he
could that he was willing to keep all that
he had promised them. Then said St
Francis : "Brother Wolf, I desire that as
thou hast pledged me thy faith to this
promise outside the gates, thou wilt pledge
me thy faith again before all the people, and
not deceive me in the promise and guarantee
which I have given for thee." Then the
wolf, lifting up his right paw, placed it in
the hand of St Francis.

Whilst this and the rest that had been
told above was taking place, there was such
joy and admiration amongst all the people,
both through devotion to the saint and
through the novelty of the miracle, and also
on account of the peace made with the wolf,
that all began to cry to heaven, praising
and blessing God for sending to them St
Francis, who by his merits had delivered
them from the jaws of the cruel beast. And

after this, the said wolf lived two years in Gubbio; and went sociably into the houses, going from door to door without doing harm to anyone or anyone doing harm to him, and was continually entertained by the people. And thus, as he went through fields and lanes never did any dog bark at him. Finally, after two years, Brother Wolf died of old age; at which the citizens grieved much; for whilst he went so gently about the town they remembered the virtue and sanctity of St Francis.

XXI—How St Francis tamed the wild Turtle-doves

A CERTAIN youth had caught one day a great number of turtle-doves; and as he was taking them to market he met St Francis, who, having a singular compassion for these gentle creatures, looked at the doves with eyes of pity, and said to the youth: "O good youth, I pray thee give me these gentle birds, to which in the Holy Scriptures chaste and humble and faithful souls are compared; and do not let them fall into the hands of cruel men who would kill them." And immediately the young man, being inspired by God, gave them all to St Francis; and he received them into his bosom, and said to them tenderly: "O my little sisters, simple, innocent and chaste doves, why have you let yourselves be snared? See, I will snatch you from death and make nests for you, wherein you may

increase and multiply according to the commandment of our Creator."

And St Francis went and made nests for them all; and they took to their nests, and began to lay eggs, and hatched them without fear before the eyes of the brothers; and they were as tame and as familiar with St Francis and all the other brothers as if they had been domestic fowls always accustomed to be fed by them; and they would not depart until St Francis with his blessing gave them leave to go. And to the young man who had given them to him, St Francis said : " Little son, thou wilt yet be a brother in this order, and wilt serve Jesus Christ nobly." And so it came to pass; for the said youth became a brother, and lived in the order in great sanctity.

XXII—How St Francis freed a Brother who was in sin

ONCE when St Francis was in prayer in the house of Portiuncula, he saw the whole place surrounded and besieged by devils as if by a great army; but not one of them could gain an entrance into the house, because the brothers there were of such great sanctity that the devils had no means of entering. But still they persevered till one day one of the brothers was angered by another, and thought within his heart what accusation he could bring against him, and how he could be revenged on him; and by this means, as this evil thought remained in the brother's mind, the devil, finding the way open to him, entered the house and placed himself on the neck of this brother.

But the holy and watchful shepherd, who was ever watching over his flock, seeing that the wolf had entered to devour his little sheep, quickly sent one to call this brother to him, and commanded him to disclose the venomous and odious thought which he had conceived against his neighbour, and by means of which he was now in the hands of the enemy. Upon which, affrighted at seeing that he was discovered by the holy father, the brother disclosed all the venomous rancour that was in him, and, acknowledging his fault, humbly begged for penance and mercy. And this done, he being now absolved from his sin and having received his penance, immediately, before the face of St Francis, the devil departed from him ; and the brother, thus freed from the cruel beast by the kindness of the good shepherd, gave thanks to God, and returned corrected and amended to the flock of the holy shepherd, wherein he continued to live in great sanctity.

XXIII—How St Francis converted the Soldan of Babylon to the Faith

ST FRANCIS, urged by zeal for the faith of Christ and by the desire of martyrdom, once on a time, with twelve of his holiest companions, crossed the sea in order to go

straight to the soldan of Babylon. And
they came to a country of the Saracens,
where the passes were guarded by men so
cruel that never a Christian who passed
that way could escape being put to death;
yet as it pleased God they were not slain,
but were captured and beaten and tightly
bound, and so led before the soldan. And
having come before him, St Francis, taught
by the Holy Ghost, preached so divinely of
the faith of Christ, for the sake of which he was
willing even to go through the fire, that the
soldan began to have a very great devotion
towards him, because of the constancy of
his faith and of the contempt of the world
which he saw in him (since he would not
take any gift though so utterly poor) and
also because of the fervour of martyrdom
which he perceived within him. And from
this time forth the soldan listened to him
willingly, and prayed him to come to him
often, and gave him and his companions
free leave to preach wheresoever it pleased
them. And he gave them a password by
using which they would be protected from
being injured by anyone.

At last St Francis, finding that he could
reap no more fruit in these parts and
warned by divine revelation, prepared to
return once more to the lands of the faithful,
he and all his companions; and they all
came together, and went for the last time to
the soldan to take leave of him. Then the
soldan said to him : "Brother Francis, I

would willingly turn to the faith of Christ, but I fear to do so now; for if the others heard of it they would kill both thee and myself and all thy companions; and I know that thou mayest still live to do much good; and I also have certain weighty matters to despatch. I would not therefore at this time bring death upon thee and upon myself. But teach me how I may be saved: I am prepared to do all that which thou wilt lay upon me." Then said St Francis: "My lord, I must now depart from thee; but after I shall have returned to my own country, and gone to heaven by God's grace after my death, according as it shall please God I will send thee two of my brothers from whom thou shalt receive the holy Baptism of Christ, and so thou shalt be saved as has been revealed to me by our Lord Jesus Christ. And do thou meanwhile keep thyself free from all that would hinder the grace of God, that when it comes to thee it may find thee prepared for faith and devotion." And this he promised to do, and did it. Having spoken thus, St Francis departed with the venerable company of his saintly companions; and after several years, by the death of the body, he gave up his soul to God.

And the soldan becoming ill and still expecting the promise of St Francis to be fulfilled, had guards placed at certain passes, and commanded that if two brothers should appear in the habit of St Francis they should forthwith be brought to him. At that very time St Francis appeared to two brothers and commanded them to go without delay to the soldan, and procure the salvation of his soul as he himself had promised. The brothers departed with haste and crossed the sea, and they were conducted by the guards to the soldan. And when he saw them he was filled with great joy, and said : "Now I know of a truth that God hath sent His servants for my salvation according to the promise which, inspired by God, St Francis made to me." Therefore he received instruction in the faith, and holy Baptism from these brothers; and thus regenerated in Christ he died of the illness from which he was then suffering, and his soul was saved by the merits and the prayers of St Francis.

XXIV—How St Francis miraculously healed the Leper

THE true disciple of Christ, St Francis, whilst still living in this miserable life, sought with all his strength to follow Christ, the perfect Master. Wherefore it came to pass many times that the souls of those whose bodies he healed, were by divine power also healed by God at one and the same hour, even as we read of Christ. Now he not only willingly served the lepers himself, but besides this had ordained that the brothers of his order, wherever they went or stayed throughout the world, should serve lepers everywhere for the

love of Christ, who for our sakes was willing
to be accounted a leper.

So it came to pass once that in a certain
place near to which St Francis then dwelt,
the brothers were serving in an infirmary for
lepers and other sick, where was one leper so
impatient and so insufferably insolent that
everyone believed for certain—and it was the
fact—that he was possessed by the devil;
because he assailed with such shameful abuse,
and so showered blows upon everyone who
served him ; and because, which was still
worse, he blasphemously reviled the blessed
Christ and His most holy Virgin Mother
Mary ; till at last no one could by any means
be found who could or would serve him.
And although the brothers strove to bear
patiently the injuries and insults levelled
against themselves, that so they might increase the merit of their patience, yet those
which were uttered against Christ and His
Mother they could not in conscience bear,
so that they determined to abandon him altogether. But they would not do this until
they had mentioned the matter, according to
the orders which they had received, to St
Francis,: who was then staying in a place
close by.

And when he had heard what they had to
tell, St Francis himself went to this perverse
leper ; and going up to him he saluted him,
saying : " God give thee peace, my beloved
brother ! " But the leper answered : " What
peace can I have from God, who has taken

away peace and all good from me, and caused
me to be covered with rottenness and to
stink?" And St Francis said: "My son,
have patience, forasmuch as the infirmities of
the body are given by God in this world for
the salvation of the soul, because they are of
great merit when borne patiently." The
sick man replied: "And how can I bear
patiently the continual pain which afflicts
me both day and night? And I am afflicted
not only by my disease, but still worse by the
brothers whom thou hast sent to serve me,
and who do not serve me as they ought."

Then St Francis, knowing by inspiration
from God that this leper was possessed by
the evil spirit, went and gave himself up to
prayer, and besought God devoutly for him.
And his prayer ended, he returned to the
leper; and said: "Now, I will serve thee myself, since thou art not contented with the
others." "As thou pleasest," said the man,
"but what canst thou do for me more than
the others?" And St Francis answered
him: "Whatever thou desirest, I will do."
Said the leper: "I desire that thou shouldst
wash me all over, because my wounds smell
so foully that I cannot bear with myself."
Then St Francis quickly had water heated,
and many sweet-smelling herbs put into it;
and after this, he stripped the leper and began
to wash him with his own hands whilst another brother poured on the water. And by
divine miracle, wherever St Francis touched
him with his holy hands the leprosy departed,

and the flesh became perfectly whole : and as the flesh began to heal, so the soul began to be healed also. Wherefore the leper, seeing that he was on the way to be healed, began to have great compunction and repentance for his sins and to weep bitterly ; so that as the body was cleansed outwardly from the leprosy by the washing with water, so the soul was purified inwardly from sin by repentance and by tears.

And being completely healed in body and in soul, he humbly acknowledged his sin, and said weeping and with a loud voice : "Woe to me, who am worthy of hell for the injuries and insults which I have put upon the brothers in words and deeds, and for my impatience and blasphemy against God!" And then for fifteen days he continued in bitter weeping over his sins, begging mercy of God ; and meanwhile he confessed all his sins to a priest. And St Francis, seeing so express a miracle which God had worked by his hands, returned thanks to God, and departed, going thence to a far country, because from humility he would fly from all glory for himself, and because in all his works he sought the honour and glory of God only and not his own.

Then, as it pleased God, the leper, healed in body and soul, after thus doing penance for fifteen days fell sick of another malady, and fortified by the sacraments of the Church he died a holy death ; and his soul, on its way to paradise, appeared in the air to St Francis

who was in a wood in prayer, and said :
" Dost thou know me again ? " " Who art
thou ? " said St Francis. " I am that leper
whom the blessed Christ healed through thy
merits ; and now I am going into life eternal,
for which I give thanks to God and to thee.
Blessed be thou in thy soul and thy body;
and blessed be thy holy words and works,
because through thee many souls will be
saved in the world ; and know that there will
never be a day while the world lasts, in which
the holy angels and all the saints will not
thank God for the blessed fruits which thou
and thy order will bring forth all over the
world; and therefore be comforted, and give
thanks to God, and may His blessing stay
with thee." And saying these words, he
went to heaven; and St Francis remained
much consoled.

XXV—How St Francis converted three Robbers that were murderers

ST FRANCIS one day was going through the
desert to St Sepulchre. And passing by a
castle called Monte Casale, there came to him
a youth, noble and delicate, who said to him :
" Father, I would very willingly be one of
your brothers." St Francis answered him :
" My son, thou art but a youth, and delicate
and noble : it may be that thou couldst not
endure our poverty and hardships." And he
said : " Father, are you not men, as I am ?
therefore as you endure them, so can I by

G

the grace of Jesus Christ." St Francis was
much pleased with this answer; therefore
blessing him, he forthwith received him into
the order, giving him the name of Brother
Angelo, where he bore himself so graciously
that within a short time St Francis made him
guardian of the house at Monte Casale.

At that time there were three noted
robbers frequenting the district, who did
much harm in the country round. These
men came one day to the said house, and
prayed the guardian, Brother Angelo, to
give them something to eat. But the
guardian reproved them harshly, answering
them thus: "You thieves and vile murderers, not ashamed to rob others of the
fruits of their labours; but more than this,
presumptuous and impudent that you are,
you would devour the alms which have
been set apart for the servants of God: you
do not even deserve that the earth should
hold you, since you respect neither man nor
God who created you; go your ways therefore, and do not show yourselves here
again:" at which they went away discon-
tented and in a rage.

And behold, St Francis came in with a
wallet of bread and a little flask of wine,
which he and his companions had begged;
and the guardian telling him how he had
driven the men away, St Francis severely
reproved him, saying that he had acted
very cruelly; because sinners can be better
brought back to God by gentleness than by

harsh reproof: whence our Master, Jesus
Christ, whose Gospel we have promised to
observe, has said that the whole need not a
physician but they that are sick; and that
He was not come to call the just, but
sinners to repentance; and therefore also
He many times ate with them. " Seeing,
therefore," said he, "that thou hast acted
contrary to charity and contrary to the
holy Gospel of Christ, I command thee, by
holy obedience, that thou immediately take
this wallet of bread and this flask of wine
which I have received, and go after them
with speed, and seek them over hill and
valley until thou find them, and give them
all this bread and wine from me; and then
kneel before them, and confess humbly thy
fault in being so harsh to them; and beg
them from me not to do any more evil, but
to fear God and not to offend Him more;
and if they will do this, I promise to provide for their wants, and to give them continually enough to eat and drink: and
when thou hast done this, return humbly to
thy place."

Whilst the guardian went to fulfil this
his command, St Francis betook himself to
prayer, entreating God to soften the hearts
of the robbers and to convert them to true
penitence. Having therefore overtaken
them, the obedient guardian gave them the
bread and wine, and did and said as St
Francis had bidden on him. And as it
pleased God, whilst the robbers were eating

the alms that St Francis had sent them, they began to say to each other : "Woe to us, miserable wretches! How hard will be the pains of hell which we must expect, who go about, not only robbing our neighbours and beating and wounding them, but even murdering also; and notwithstanding so many evil and shameful deeds that we have done, we have had no remorse of conscience nor fear of God; and see how this holy brother who came to us but now, for a few words justly spoken against our wickedness, humbly owned himself in fault, and besides this brought us bread and wine and so liberal a promise from the holy father. Verily these are holy brothers and men of God who merit paradise; and we are the sons of eternal perdition who merit the pains of hell, and every day increase our condemnation; and we know not, after all the sins we have committed up till now, if we can return to the mercy of God."

Such and similar words one of them said to the others, who answered, "For sure thou sayest the truth, but hearken, what can we do?" "Let us go," said one, "to holy Francis; and if he gives us hope that we may find mercy with God for our sins, let us do what he commands us, and perhaps we may be able to deliver our souls from the pains of hell." This counsel pleased the others; therefore all three being agreed, they went in haste to St

Francis, and said to him: "Father, for the many shameful sins which we have done, we cannot believe that it is possible for us to return to the mercy of God; but if thou hast any hope that God would receive us to His mercy, behold we are ready to do thy bidding and to do penance with thee." Then St Francis, receiving them charitably and with benignity, comforted them with many examples; and, assuring them of the mercy of God, promised them for certain that they should obtain it, and showed them that the mercy of God was infinite, and that if we had sins without number yet the mercy of God is greater than our sins according to the Holy Gospel; and the Apostle St Paul has said: "Christ the blessed came into the world to save sinners." Instructed by these and the like words, the said three robbers renounced the devil and his works, and St Francis received them into the order, and they began to do great penance, and two of them lived but a short time after their conversion, and went to paradise.

But the third surviving, and looking back on his sins, gave himself to do such penance that for fifteen years continually, except during the Lent which he kept in common with the other brothers, he fasted three days in the week on bread and water, and went always barefoot with nothing on his back but a tunic, and never slept after matins.

About this time, St Francis departed from this miserable life. And having now for many years continued in such penance, behold there came to the aforesaid thief one night, after matins, so great a temptation to sleep that he could not resist the inclination nor remain watching as he ought. Finally, being neither able to resist sleep any longer nor to pray, he went to his bed in order to rest himself; but no sooner had he laid down his head, than he was ravished and led in spirit away unto a very high mountain in which was a most profound precipice, and on this side and on that sharp and splintered rocks and broken ledges projecting from the rocks, so that the precipice was fearful to behold. And the angel who was leading this brother pushed him on, and threw him down over the precipice, where, tumbling and rebounding from rock to rock and from stone to stone, he at last arrived at the bottom of the precipice all dismembered and broken to pieces, as it seemed to him. And as he lay thus on the ground in evil plight, he that led him said to him: "Rise up, for thou must make still a greater journey." And the brother answered: "Thou seemst to me a very indiscreet and cruel man who, seeing me lying here almost dead from the fall which has so broken me, yet tellest me to rise." And the angel approaching him touched him, and healed all his limbs, and restored him.

And after this, the angel showed him a

great plain full of sharp and cutting stones
and thorns and brambles, and said to him
that it behoved him to traverse the whole of
this plain, and that he must pass over it
barefooted until he came to the end, where
he perceived a fiery furnace into which he
must enter.   And the brother having passed
over this plain with great pain and anguish,
the angel said to him : " Enter into this
furnace, for it behoves thee so to do." And
he answered: " Alas! how cruel a guide
thou art to me, who, seeing me near to
death through the agonizing journey over
this plain, biddest me now for rest to enter
this fiery furnace! " And looking he saw
round about the furnace many devils with
iron forks in their hands, with which, while
he hesitated to enter, they forced him in.

And when he had entered the furnace,
looking about, he saw one that had been his
fellow who was all on fire ; and he asked
him : " O unhappy companion, how camest
thou hither?" And the other replied :
"Go on a little further, and thou wilt
find my wife, thy kinswoman, who will tell
thee the cause of our damnation." The
brother went further in, and behold this said
kinswoman appeared all blazing, shut up in
a corn measure all aflame ; and he asked
her : " O unhappy and miserable cousin,
wherefore hast thou come into this cruel
torment ?" And she answered: " Because
at the time of the great famine, which was
foretold by holy Francis, my husband and I

falsified the measure of the wheat and the grain which we sold ; and therefore I burn here, shut up in this corn-measure."

And after these words, the angel who was leading the brother thrust him out from the furnace, and said to him : " Prepare thyself to make a terrible journey which thou hast yet before thee." And he, bitterly lamenting, said : " O most hard conductor who hast no compassion on me ! Thou seest that I am almost burnt up in this furnace, and yet again thou wouldst lead me on a perilous and horrible journey." And the angel touched him, and made him whole and strong. And he led him to a bridge, which could not be passed without great danger, because it was exceedingly frail and narrow, and very slippery and without a railing at the sides. And beneath it flowed a terrible stream, full of serpents and dragons and scorpions, and casting forth an exceeding great stench.

And the angel said to him : " Pass over this bridge, for thou must needs do so." And he answered : " How can I pass over it without falling into this perilous stream ? " And the angel said : "Follow me, and place thy foot where thou shalt see I place mine, and thou shalt pass over it well." The brother crossed over therefore, behind the angel, as he had instructed him, until they came to the middle of the bridge : and having come to the middle, the angel flew away, and departed from him, and

went to a very high mountain afar off on
the other side of the bridge.   And the
brother saw well which way the angel had
gone, but remaining without a guide, and
looking down below, where he saw those
terrible animals with their heads stretched
out of the water, and with their jaws open
ready to devour him if perchance he should
fall, he was seized with such fear and
trembling that he nowise knew what to say
or what to do, because he could neither
turn back nor go onwards.   Wherefore,
seeing himself in such great tribulation and
that he had no refuge save in God, he lay
down, and, holding on to the bridge with
his arms, with all his heart and with tears he
recommended himself to God, that of His
most holy mercy He would succour him.

And as his prayer ended, it seemed to
him that he began to put forth wings,
whence he began with great joy to hope
that they would grow so that he might be
able to fly from where he was on the bridge
to the place where the angel had flown.
But after a time, from the great desire he
had to get over this bridge, he began to fly ;
and because his wings were not long
enough, he fell down on the bridge, and
the feathers drooped ; wherefore he embraced the bridge as before, and recommended himself to God as at the first.

And having prayed, again he seemed to
put forth wings ; but, as before, he did not
wait till they were perfectly grown, so that,

attempting to fly before the time, he fell as before on the bridge, and the feathers drooped. Therefore, seeing that by reason of the haste he was in to fly before the time he fell each time, he began to say with himself: " Of a surety, if I put forth wings again the third time, I will wait long enough until they are grown, so that I may be able to fly without falling again." And remaining in this thought, he found himself the third time putting forth wings, and waited a long time, even until they were well grown, so that it seemed to him that, with the first and second and third putting forth of his wings, he had waited a good hundred and fifty years or more.

At the last he raised himself the third time, and with all his strength he took his flight, and flew up on high, even to the place where the angel had flown. And knocking at the door of the palace in which the angel was, the door-keeper asked of him: " Who art thou that comest here?" He answered: " I am a Friar Minor." The porter said to him: " Wait, for I will bring St Francis to see if he know thee." While he was going for St Francis, the other began to consider the wonderful walls of this palace, and lo! they seemed translucent, and of such brightness that he saw clearly the choirs of the saints and all that was being done within.

And standing thus stupefied at what he beheld, behold there came St Francis, with Brother Bernard and Brother Giles, and

after them such a multitude of saints and
holy women who had followed his example,
that they seemed almost innumerable: and
being come to the gate, St Francis said to
the porter: "Let him come in, for he is one
of my friars." And immediately he entered,
he felt such consolation and sweetness that
he forgot all the tribulations he had
suffered, as though they had never been.
Upon which, St Francis leading him within,
showed him many marvellous things, and
afterwards said to him : "Son, thou must
needs return to the world and remain there
seven days, during which prepare thyself
diligently with great devotion ; for after the
seven days are ended I will come for thee,
and then thou shalt enter with me into this
place of the blessed."

St Francis was arrayed in a marvellous
mantle adorned with most beautiful stars,
and his five stigmas were like unto five
most beautiful stars and of such splendour
that all the palace was illumined with their
rays. And Brother Bernard had on his
head a crown of most beautiful stars, and
Brother Giles was adorned with a most
marvellous light, and many other holy friars
he recognized amongst them, whom he had
never seen in the world. Having taken
leave therefore of St Francis, he returned,
although much against his will, to the
world ; and awaking and coming to himself,
the brothers were ringing for prime; so that
he was in that vision only from matins until

prime, although it seemed to him many years. And having recounted to his guardian the whole of this vision in order, as it befel him, within seven days after he sickened of a fever; and on the eighth day, St Francis according to his promise came to him, with a very great multitude of glorious saints, and led forth his soul to the kingdom of the blessed, and to eternal life.

XXVI—How St Francis converted two Scholars at Bologna

As St Francis came once on a time to the city of Bologna, all the townsfolk ran out to see him; and so great was the crowding of the people, that with great difficulty could they reach the great square. And the square being full of men and women and of scholars, St Francis stood up in the midst of them on a raised place, and preached as the Holy Ghost inspired him; and he preached so wonderfully that it seemed as though it were an angel rather than a man who was preaching. And his words appeared so heavenly that they were as sharp darts which pierced the breasts of those that heard him, so that during his preaching a great multitude of men and women were converted to repentance.

Amongst these there were two noble students of the March of Ancona; one was called Pellegrino and the other Rinieri, both of whom were so touched to the heart

by the divine inspiration through the aforesaid preaching that they came to St Francis,
and said to him that they desired to abandon the world entirely, and to be of the
number of his brethren.   Then St Francis,
considering their great fervour, and knowing by revelation that they were sent by
God and that they would lead a holy life in
the order, received them with joy, saying :
" Thou, Pellegrino, keep the way of
humility in the order ; and do thou, Brother
Rinieri, serve the brethren."   And so it
was ; for Brother Pellegrino never would be
a cleric, but became one of the lay brothers,
although he was very learned and profoundly versed in the canon law ; by which
humility he attained to great perfection of
virtue, insomuch that Brother Bernard, the
first-born of St Francis, said of him that he
was one of the most perfect friars in this
world.   And finally, the said Brother Pellegrino, full of virtue, closed his blessed life
on earth, performing many miracles both
before and after his death.   And likewise
Brother Rinieri devotedly and faithfully
served the brothers, living in great holiness
and humility, and he became very familiar·
with St Francis.   And being made afterwards minister of the province of the March
of Ancona, he ruled it during a long time
with the greatest peace and discretion.
    After a while it pleased God to permit
a very great temptation to arise in his soul;
for which cause, being in much trouble and

anguish, he afflicted himself greatly with fasting and discipline, with tears and prayers, day and night. Nevertheless he could not banish the temptation, but oftentimes was greatly discouraged because he reputed himself abandoned of God. Being in this plight therefore, as a last remedy he determined to go to St Francis, thinking thus within himself: " If St Francis shows me a good countenance, and is familiar with me as is his wont, I will believe that God will yet have pity on me; but if not, it will be a sign that I am abandoned of God."

Therefore he departed, and went to St Francis, who was sick and sojourning at that time in the palace of the bishop of Assisi; and God revealed to him all the manner of the temptation that had come to the said Brother Rinieri, and his disposition, and how he was coming to him. And immediately St Francis called Brother Leo and Brother Masseo, and said to them: " Go with speed to meet my most dearly beloved son, Brother Rinieri, embrace him for me, and salute him, and say to him that of all the brothers that are in the world I love him singularly." They went therefore, and found Brother Rinieri on the way, and embracing him told him that which St Francis had commanded them; whence such consolation and sweetness came into his soul that he was as one beside himself, and thanking God with all his heart he went on till he arrived at the place where

St Francis lay ill. And although St Francis was suffering from grievous infirmity, nevertheless, when he heard Brother Rinieri coming, he arose and went to meet him, and most sweetly embraced him, and said to him : " My dearest son, Brother Rinieri, of all the brothers that are in the world I love thee singularly." And having thus said, he made the sign of the most holy cross on his forehead, and kissed him, and again he said to him: "Dearest son, this temptation has been permitted by God for thy great gain of merit, but if thou dost not wish to have this gain any longer do not have it." O wonder! Scarcely had St Francis pronounced these words than immediately all the temptation left him, as if he had never in his whole life felt it, and he remained entirely consoled.

XXVII—Of the Rapture that came to Brother Bernard

THIS great favour God oftentimes granted the poor evangelicals, who had abandoned the world for the love of Christ; and especially showed forth in Brother Bernard of Quintavalle, who after he had taken the habit of St Francis was many times ravished in God by the contemplation of heavenly things. Amongst other things, it happened once, that being in church hearing Mass with his mind raised to God, he became so absorbed and ravished in God that when the

Body of Christ was being elevated he perceived nothing, neither did he kneel nor take down his hood as the others did. Looking fixedly, but without any motion of his eyes, he remained from morning until noon unconscious, and after mid-day, returning to himself, he went about the place crying out with a voice full of admiration : " O brothers ! O brothers ! O brothers ! there is not a man in this country, were he ever so great and so noble, who, if there were promised to him a palace most beautiful and full of gold, would not willingly carry a sackful of dung in order to gain so noble a treasure."

The aforesaid Brother Bernard had his mind so elevated to this heavenly treasure promised to those who love God, that for fifteen years continually he went with his mind and his face raised to heaven ; in which time he never satisfied his hunger at table, although he always ate a little of what was placed before him ; because he said that a man does not attain perfect abstinence in that which he does not relish, but the true abstinence is temperance in that which is pleasant to the palate. From this abstinence there came to him also such light and illumination of the intelligence that even the great clerics had recourse to him for the solution of the hardest questions and the most obscure passages of Scripture, and he solved every difficulty.

And because his mind was entirely free

and detached from earthly things he, like
the swallows, flew high up by contemplation,
so that sometimes for twenty days, sometimes for thirty days, he remained alone on
the tops of the highest mountains in the contemplation of heavenly things.   Wherefore
Brother Giles said of him that to no other
man was given this gift which was given to
Brother Bernard of Quintavalle, namely,
that he should feed flying like the swallow;
and on account of this excellent favour which
he had received from God, St Francis willingly and often spoke with him both day and
night; so that sometimes they were found
together ravished in God the whole night
long in the wood, where they had retired to
speak together of the things of God.

XXVIII—How the Devil appeared in the form
    of the Crucified on several occasions to
    Brother Ruffino, telling him that all the
    good he did was lost

BROTHER RUFFINO, one of the most noble
citizens of the town of Assisi, a companion
of St Francis and a man of great sanctity,
was at one time most powerfully assaulted
and tempted in his soul about predestination;
through which he became full of melancholy
and sadness, because the devil put it into his
heart that he was damned and not of those
predestined to eternal life, and that he would
lose that which he did in the order.   And
this temptation lasting day after day,

H

through shame he did not reveal it to St
Francis; nevertheless he did not omit to pray
and use the customary abstinence, for which
cause the enemy began to add to him sorrow
upon sorrow over and above the battle
within, assaulting him with false apparitions.
Wherefore he appeared to him at one time
in the form of the Crucified, and said to him:
" O Brother Ruffino, wherefore dost thou
afflict thyself with penance and prayer, since
thou art not of the number of those elected
to eternal life? and believe me that I know
whom I have elected and predestinated, and
do not believe the son of Peter Bernardone
if he tells thee the contrary; and also do not
ask him about this matter, because neither
he nor anyone knows it if not I, who am the
Son of God: and therefore believe me for
certain that thou art of the number of the
damned, and the son of Peter Bernardone,
thy father, and his father also are damned,
and whosoever follows him is deceived."
And these words said, Brother Ruffino began
to be so disheartened by the prince of darkness that he lost all faith and love he had
had for St Francis, and did not care to tell
him anything.

But that which Brother Ruffino did not
tell the holy father the Holy Ghost revealed
to him: wherefore St Francis, seeing in
spirit such peril to the said brother, sent
Brother Masseo for him, whom Brother
Ruffino answered roughly: " What have I
to do with Brother Francis?" Then Brother
Masseo, all filled with the divine wisdom,

knowing the deception of the devil, said:
"O Brother Ruffino, dost thou not know
that Brother Francis is like an angel of God,
who has illumined so many souls in the
world, and through whom we have received
the grace of God? therefore I will have thee
come with me without delay to him, because
I clearly see that thou art deceived by the
devil." And this said, Brother Ruffino
arose and went to St Francis. And St
Francis seeing him coming from afar, began
to cry out: "O naughty Brother Ruffino,
whom hast thou believed?" And when
Brother Ruffino was come to him, he told
him in order all the temptations that he
had from the devil, both within and without,
and showed him clearly that he who had
appeared to him was the devil and not
Christ, and that on no account should he
consent to his suggestions; "but when the
devil shall say to thee again: 'Thou art
damned,' answer him: 'Open thy mouth.'
And this shalt be the sign to thee that he is
the devil and not Christ: as soon as thou
shalt have given him this answer, immediately he will fly. Again, by this token thou
shouldst know that this was the devil, because he hardened thy heart against all
good, which thing it is his proper office to
do; but Christ the blessed never hardens
the heart of the faithful man, but rather
softens it, as he hast said by the mouth of the
prophet: 'I will take away the heart of
stone, and give them a heart of flesh.'"

Then Brother Ruffino, seeing that St

Francis told him in order all the manner of his temptation, and melted by his words, began to weep abundantly, to give praise to St Francis, and humbly acknowledge his fault in having hidden his temptation. And thus he remained all consoled and comforted by the admonitions of the holy father, and all changed for the better. Then finally St Francis said to him: " Go, son, and confess, and do not cease with diligence to pray as usual; and know that assuredly this temptation shalt be of great use and consolation to thee, and in a short time thou shalt prove it."

Having returned therefore to his cell in the wood, and continuing in prayer with many tears, behold, the enemy came to Brother Ruffino in the form of Christ as to his outward appearance, and said to him: "O Brother Ruffino, did not I say to thee that thou shouldst not believe the son of Peter Bernardone, and that thou shouldst not weary thyself with tears and prayers, seeing that thou art damned? What doth it benefit thee to afflict thyself during life, and then when thou diest thou shalt be damned?" And suddenly Brother Ruffino answered the devil: "Open thy mouth." At which the devil, disgusted, immediately departed, with such a storm and commotion of the stones on Mount Sabassio, which was near by, that for a great space there remained the ruins of the stones which fell down; and so great was the striking of one against

another in their rolling that they kindled
terrible flashes of fire through the valley;
and at the horrible noise which they made
St Francis and his companions came out of
the house with great amazement to see what
marvel had happened ; and even to this day
is seen there that immense ruin of stones.

Then Brother Ruffino manifestly saw
that it was the devil who had deceived him.
And turning to St Francis, he threw himself again on the ground, and acknowledged
his fault; and St Francis comforted him
with gentle words, and sent him all consoled
to his cell, in which as he remained in most
devout prayer, Christ the blessed appeared
to him, and inflamed his whole soul with the
divine love, and said : "Well hast thou done,
son, that thou hast believed Brother Francis,
because he that distressed thee was the
devil; but I am Christ, thy Master, and to
make thee well assured of it I give thee this
sign : as long as thou livest thou shalt feel
no more sadness or melancholy." And
having thus said, Christ departed, leaving
him so much joy and sweetness of spirit and
elevation of mind that day and night he was
absorbed and ravished in God.

And from that time he was so confirmed
in grace, and so sure of his salvation that
he was entirely changed into another man,
and would have remained day and night in
prayer and in the contemplation of divine
things, if the others would have let him
remain.   Wherefore St Francis said of him

that Brother Ruffino had been canonized in
this life by Christ, and that, except in his
own presence, he would not hesitate to call
him St Ruffino, although he was still living
upon the earth.

XXIX—Of the beautiful Sermon preached in Assisi by St Francis and Brother Ruffino

BROTHER RUFFINO by continued contemplation was so absorbed in God that he became
almost insensible and speechless, and moreover had neither grace nor courage nor
eloquence in preaching; nevertheless St
Francis commanded him one day to go to
Assisi and preach to the people that which
God inspired him to say.   To which Brother
Ruffino replied: "Reverend Father, I pray
you to excuse me and send me not, because,
as thou knowest, I have not the grace of
preaching but am simple and stupid."   And
St Francis said: "Since thou hast not
obeyed promptly, I command thee by holy
obedience that thou go in thy breeches only
to Assisi, and enter into a church, and preach
to the people."   At this command, Brother
Ruffino stripped off his habit and went to
Assisi, and entered a church; and, having
made his reverence to the altar, he ascended
the pulpit and began to preach, at which the
children and the men began to laugh, and
said: "Now see, these men do so much penance that they become fools and beside themselves."

In the meanwhile St Francis, thinking

over the prompt obedience of Brother Ruffino,
who was one of the highest gentlemen of
Assisi, and of the hard command which he
had given him, began to reproach himself,
saying: "Whence hast thou so great presumption, son of Peter Bernardone, thou sorry
wight, to command Brother Ruffino, who is
one of the highest gentlemen of Assisi, to go
and preach to the people as if he were a madman? By God's grace, thou shalt prove in
thyself that which thou hast commanded to
others." And immediately, in fervour of
spirit, he stripped himself in like manner,
and went his way to Assisi, taking with him
Brother Leo to carry his habit and that of
Brother Ruffino. And the townsmen of
Assisi, seeing him in the same plight, derided him, declaring him and Brother Ruffino
both mad through excess of penance.

And St Francis entered the church, where
Brother Ruffino was preaching in these
words: "O most dearly beloved, fly the world
and forsake sin; restore that which belongs
to others if you would escape hell; keep the
commandments of God by loving God and
your neighbour if you wish to go to heaven;
do penance if you would possess the kingdom
of heaven." Then St Francis ascended the
pulpit and began to preach so wondrously of
the contempt of the world, of holy penance,
of voluntary poverty and of the desire of the
heavenly kingdom and of the nakedness and
opprobrium of the Passion of our Lord Jesus
Christ, that all they that were present at the

sermon, both men and women, a great multitude, began to weep bitterly, with great devotion and compunction of heart. And not only in the church but through all Assisi that day there was such weeping for the Passion of Christ that the like was never known.

And the people being thus edified and consoled by this act of St Francis and Brother Ruffino, St Francis re-clothed Brother Ruffino and himself, and thus rehabited they returned to the convent of the Portiuncula, praising and glorifying God who had given them grace to overcome themselves by the contempt of themselves, and to edify the little sheep of Christ by a good example, and to show how much the world is to be despised. And in that day the devotion of the people increased so greatly towards them that he reputed himself blessed who could touch the hem of their garment.

XXX—How St Francis knew the secrets of the consciences of all his Friars

As our Lord Jesus Christ says in the Gospel: "I know My sheep and they know Me:" so the blessed father, St Francis, as a good shepherd, knew by divine revelation all the merits and virtues of his companions, and so he knew their defects ; for which reason he knew how to apply the best remedy for such, namely, by humbling the proud, exalting the humble, reproving vice and praising virtue, as is to be seen in the admirable revelations

which he had concerning his primitive family.
Amongst these we find that St Francis,
being with the said family in a certain place
discoursing of God, and Brother Ruffino not
being with them in this discourse, but being
in the wood in contemplation whilst they
continued reasoning of God—behold, Brother
Ruffino came out of the wood, and passed by
at a little distance from them.

Then St Francis, seeing him, turned to his
companions and asked them, " Who, think
you, is the holiest soul that God has in the
world ? " And they answered him saying
that they thought it was his own. Then St
Francis said : " Most beloved brothers, I am
of myself the most unworthy and the vilest
man that God has in this world ; but see you
that Brother Ruffino who hast just now come
out of the wood ? God has revealed to me
that his soul is one of the three most holy
souls in the world ; and of a surety I tell you
that I should not hesitate to call him St
Ruffino in his lifetime, for his soul is confirmed in grace and sanctified and canonized
in heaven by our Lord Jesus Christ:" but
these words St Francis never spoke in the
presence of the said Brother Ruffino.

In like manner, as St Francis knew the
faults of his brethren, he clearly saw through
Brother Elias whom he oftentimes reproved
for his pride ; and also Brother John della
Capella, of whom he foretold that he would
hang himself by the neck ; and that brother
whom the devil held tightly by the throat,

when he was corrected for his disobedience ;
and many other brethren whose secret defects
and virtues he clearly knew by the revelations of Christ.

XXXI—How Brother Masseo obtained from Christ the virtue of his Humility

THE first companions of St Francis with all
their strength endeavoured to be poor in the
things of this world, and rich in virtues by
which we attain to the true heavenly and
eternal riches. It came to pass one day
that, being gathered together speaking of
God, one of them spoke thus by way of
example. There was one who was a great
friend of God, and who had great grace both
for the active and for the contemplative life,
and, moreover, had such an excessive humility that he reputed himself the greatest
sinner ; the which humility sanctified and
confirmed him in grace, and made him continually to grow in virtue and in the gifts of
God, and never suffered him to fall into sin.
Brother Masseo, hearing such wonderful
things of humility, and knowing it to be a
treasure of eternal life, began to be so inflamed with the love and the desire of this
virtue of humility that, in great fervour raising his face to heaven, he made a vow and
firm resolve never to rejoice again in this
world except in so far as he should feel this
virtue to be perfectly in his soul. And from
that time forth he remained almost entirely
secluded within his cell, macerating his body

with fastings, vigils, and prayers, and very
great abundance of tears before God in order
to obtain this virtue, without which he reputed himself worthy of hell, and with which
that friend of God, of whom he had heard,
was so dowered.

And remaining in this desire many
days, Brother Masseo entered one day into
the wood, and in fervour of spirit he went
through it shedding tears, sending forth
sighs and cries, asking from God with
fervent desire this divine virtue. And
because God willingly grants the prayers of
the humble and contrite, as Brother
Masseo was standing thus, there came a
voice from heaven which called him twice :
" Brother Masseo ! Brother Masseo ! " And
he, knowing in spirit that it was the
voice of Christ, answered : " My Lord ! "
And Christ said to him : " What wouldst
thou give to have this grace which thou
hast asked ? " Brother Masseo answered :
" Lord, I would give the eyes out of my
head." And Christ said to him : " And I
will that thou have the grace, and thine eyes
also." And this said, the voice ceased.

And Brother Masseo remained filled
with so much grace with the virtue he had
desired and with the light of God that from
this time forth he was ever in mirth and
gladness ; and oftentimes when he prayed
he expressed his gladness of heart in the
form of a sound like that of a dove uttering
Coo, Coo, Coo. And with a merry counten-

ance and a joyous heart he remained thus
in contemplation : and along with this,
having become altogether most humble, he
reputed himself the least of all men upon
earth. Being asked by Brother James of
Fallerone why, in his rejoicing, he did not
change his tune, he replied with great delight that when one was well contented in one
thing there was no need of change of tune.

XXXII—How St Clare by command of the
    Pope blessed the loaves which were on the
    table

ST CLARE, most devoted disciple of the
cross of Christ and noble plant of St
Francis, was of such sanctity that not only
bishops and cardinals but the pope himself
desired with great affection to see her, to
hear her, and oftentimes visited her in person.
Amongst other times once, when the Holy
Father went to her convent to hear her
speak of heavenly and divine things, whilst
they were together holding divers dis-
courses, St Clare meanwhile had the tables
prepared and the loaves placed on them in
order that the Holy Father might bless
them. The spiritual discourse being ended,
she inclined herself with great reverence,
prayed him to be pleased to bless the loaves
before the repast. The Holy Father
answered : " Sister Clare, most true and
faithful one, I desire that thou bless these
loaves, and make on them the sign of the

most holy cross to which thou hast entirely
given thyself." St Clare replied: "Most
Holy Father, pardon me who would be
worthy of too great rebuke if before the
vicar of Christ I, who am a worthless
woman, should presume to give this blessing." And the pope answered: "In order
that this may not be imputed to presumption but to the merit of obedience, I command thee, by holy obedience, that thou
make on these loaves the sign of the most
holy cross and bless them in the name of
God." Then St Clare, like a true daughter
of obedience, most devoutly blessed these
loaves with the sign of the most holy cross.
Wonderful to relate! immediately there
appeared on all these loaves the sign of the
cross most beautifully figured; then of these
loaves some were eaten, and some were
miraculously preserved. And the Holy
Father, having seen the miracle, took of the
loaves with him, and departed, leaving St
Clare with his blessing.

At that time there dwelt in the convent
Sister Ortolana, the mother of St Clare, and
Sister Agnes, her own sister full of virtue
and of the Holy Spirit, and many other
religious; to whom St Francis sent many
sick and infirm, and they, by their prayers
and by the sign of the most holy cross,
restored health to them all.

XXXIII—How St Louis, King of France, came to visit Brother Giles

ST LOUIS, king of France, went on pilgrimage to visit the holy places all over the world : and, hearing the exceeding great fame of the sanctity of Brother Giles, who was one of the companions of St Francis, he proposed in his heart and determined at all costs to visit him personally; for which reason he came to Perugia, where the said Brother Giles lived at that time. And coming to the door of the community house, as a poor unknown pilgrim with but few companions, he asked with great instance for Brother Giles, not telling the porter who he was that asked. The porter therefore went to Brother Giles, and told him there was a pilgrim at the door asking for him : and God inspired him and revealed to him that it was the king of France : wherefore immediately, with great fervour of spirit, he came out of his cell, and ran to the door; and without further questioning and without even having seen each other before, with the greatest devotion inclining themselves, they embraced, and kissed one another with such familiarity as though for a long while they had been together in intimate friendship : but with all this neither one nor the other spoke. But they stood thus embracing each other with this sign of the love of charity between them in silence. And after they had stood thus

a great space without either speaking a word
to the other, they departed from each other,
and St Louis went his way on his journey,
and Brother Giles returned to his cell.

When the king was gone, one of the
brothers asked another of his companions
who he was who had been so long embracing
Brother Giles : and the other answered
that it Louis, king of France, who had come
to see Brother Giles. Which, when he had
heard, the first brother told all the others,
and they were greatly grieved that Brother
Giles had not spoken a word to him ; and
complaining, they said to him : " O
Brother Giles, why hast thou shown thyself
so unmannerly when so holy a king hast
come from France to see thee and to hear
some good word from thy holy mouth, that
thou hast not spoken to him at all ?"

And Brother Giles answered : " Beloved
brothers, wonder not at this, for neither
could I speak a word to him nor he to me;
because, as soon as we embraced each other,
the light of wisdom revealed and manifested
his heart to me, and mine to him : and thus
by the divine operation looking into each
other's heart, we knew much better what I
would have said to him and he would have
said to me than if we had spoken it with
the mouth, and with more consolation than
if we had gone about to explain with the
voice that which we felt in our hearts.
For, from the defectiveness of human language which cannot clearly express the

mysterious secrets of God, we should much
more readily have discouraged than encour-
aged one another : and therefore know that
the king took leave of me marvellously
contented and comforted in his soul."

XXXIV—How St Clare being sick was
    miraculously carried to the Church and
    there heard the Office

ST CLARE was very sick once on a time, so
that she could not go to say the office in the
church with other religious. And the day
having come for the solemnity of the
Nativity of Christ, all the others went to
matins ; and she remained in bed, sad at
heart that she could not go with the others
to have some spiritual consolation. But
Jesus Christ her spouse, not willing to
leave her thus disconsolate, caused her to
be miraculously carried to the church of St
Francis to be present during the whole of
the office of matins and of the midnight
mass, and besides this to receive the holy
communion, and then to be carried back to
her bed.

· The religious returning to St Clare,
when the office in St Damian's was over,
said to her : " O Mother, Sister Clare, what
consolation we have had in this holy feast
of the Nativity ! would that it pleased God
you had been with us." And Sister Clare
answered : " Praise and thanks be to our
blessed Lord Jesus Christ, my sisters and

most beloved daughters; because that in
the solemnity of this most holy night, and
more even than you, I also had part with
great consolation of heart; since, by the pro-
curing of my father St Francis, and by the
grace of our Lord Jesus Christ, I have been
present in the church of my venerable
father St Francis, and with my bodily ease
and the ease of my mind also, I have heard
all the office and the playing of the organ
they have there, and have myself received
the holy Communion. Therefore, for such
a grace done me, praise and thank our Lord
Jesus Christ."

XXXV—How St Francis explained to Brother Leo a wonderful Vision that he had seen

ONCE St Francis was grievously sick, and
Brother Leo was serving him. And as the
said Brother Leo remained in prayer by the
side of St Francis, he was rapt in ecstasy,
and taken away in spirit to where there was
a very great stream, wide and impetuous.
And as he stood looking what would come
to pass, he saw some of the brothers enter
the stream bearing loads on their shoulders,
who immediately were thrown down by the
impetuosity of the stream and drowned.
Some advanced as far as a third part of the
way across, some got as far as mid-stream,
some nearly to the further bank; all of
whom, through the impetuosity of the
stream and the loads they carried on their
backs, finally slipped down and sank.

T

Seeing this, Brother Leo was filled with the greatest compassion; and suddenly, whilst he thus stood, behold there came a great multitude of brothers without any burden, and loaded with nothing which did not shine with the glory of holy poverty; and entering the stream, they passed across without any peril. And when he had seen this, Brother Leo returned to himself. Then St Francis, feeling in spirit that Brother Leo had seen some vision, called him to him and asked of him what he had seen. And when Brother Leo had told him all the vision in order, St Francis said: "What thou hast seen is true. The great stream is this world; the brothers who were drowned in the stream are those who have not followed the evangelical profession, and especially unto uttermost poverty: but they who passed over without danger are those brothers who neither seek nor possess in this world aught that is earthly or carnal, but having only that which is necessary for food and clothing, are therewith content, following Christ naked on the cross, and bearing the burden and the sweet yoke of Christ and of most holy obedience joyfully and willingly; therefore they pass with ease from this temporal life to the life eternal."

XXXVI—How Jesus Christ, at the prayer of
St Francis, converted a rich and noble
Knight

ST FRANCIS, the servant of Christ, came
late one evening to the house of a great
and powerful nobleman, who received with
hospitality both him and his companion
and treated them as though they had been
angels of God with the greatest courtesy
and devotion. For which cause St Francis
bore him great love, seeing that at their
entering the house he had embraced them
as friends and kissed them, and then
washed and wiped their feet and kissed
them humbly, and had lit a great fire and
prepared the table with many good things,
and whilst they supped continually served
them with a joyful countenance.

Now when St Francis and his companion had eaten, this nobleman said:
"Behold, my father, I offer thee myself and
my possessions: whenever you have need of
tunics or mantles or of anything whatever,
buy them, and I will pay for them; and
see, I am ready to provide for all your
wants, as by the grace of God I can, seeing
I abound in all temporal goods; and therefore, for the love of God who has given
them to me, I gladly do good to his poor."
Whence St Francis, seeing so much
courtesy and good will in him and the
largeness of his offer, conceived so much
love for him that when he was departing,

as he went he said to his companion:
"Verily this nobleman, who is so mindful
of and grateful towards God and so loving
and courteous towards his neighbours and
the poor, would do well for our religious
life and our company. Know, most dearly
beloved brother, that courtesy is one of the
properties of God, who gives His sun and
rain to the just and the unjust by courtesy;
and courtesy is the sister of charity, by
which hatred is extinguished and love is
cherished. Because I have seen so much
divine virtue in this man I would gladly
have him for a companion; and therefore I
desire that we return one day to him, and
perhaps God may have touched his heart to
wish to accompany us in the service of
God; and meanwhile we will pray God to
put this desire into his heart and to give
him the grace to carry it into effect."

Wonderful to say, a few days after St
Francis had made his prayer, God put the
desire into the heart of this nobleman; and
St Francis said to his companion: "Let us
go, my brother, to the house of our courteous host, for I have an assured hope in God
that with the same courtesy he has in
temporal things he will give himself to us
and be our companion." And they went.
And coming near to the house, St Francis
said to his companion: "Wait for me a
little; for I will first pray to God that He
would prosper our way, and that it would
please Jesus Christ to concede to us, poor
and weak as we are, the noble prey which

we think to snatch from the world by the virtue of His most holy Passion." And having thus said, he disposed himself to prayer in a place where he might be seen by the said courteous man.

Now, as it pleased God, looking hither and thither he saw St Francis standing in prayer most devoutly before Christ, who in great brightness appeared to him in this his prayer and stood before him; and standing thus he saw St Francis lifted bodily above the earth for a good space. By which thing he was so touched and inspired of God to forsake the world that immediately he came forth from his palace. And in fervour of spirit he ran towards St Francis, and coming up to him as he remained in prayer, knelt at his feet, and with great instance and devotion he prayed that it would please him to receive him to do penance with those of his company. Then St Francis, seeing that his prayer was heard of God and that this nobleman asked with great instance what he himself desired, lifted him up and in fervour and joy of spirit embraced and kissed him, most devoutly returning thanks to God who had added such an accomplished knight to his company. And the nobleman said to him : "What dost thou command me to do, my father? Behold I am ready to do thy bidding, and to give to the poor whatever I possess and to follow Christ with thee, thus disburdened of all temporal things."

And thus he did by the counsel of St

Francis, distributing what he had to the poor; and entered the order, and lived in great penitence and holiness of life and virtuous conversation.

✿

XXXVII—How St Francis knew in spirit that Brother Elias was damned, and was to die out of the order; for which cause he prayed for him, and his prayer was answered

As St Francis and Brother Elias were dwelling once in a place together, it was revealed by God to St Francis that Brother Elias was damned, and was to apostatize, and finally to die out of the order. For which cause St Francis conceived so great an aversion from him that he could never converse with him, nor speak to him; and if it happened at any time that Brother Elias went towards him, he turned another way, and went elsewhere to avoid meeting him; so that Brother Elias began to perceive and to understand that St Francis was displeased with him. Therefore, wishing to know the cause he accosted St Francis one day, wishing to speak with him, and, St Francis still turning away from him, he gently held him back by force, and began courteously to entreat him that it would please him to reveal the cause why he shunned his company, and avoided speaking with him.

And St Francis answered him: " The cause is this: because it has been revealed

to me by God that for thy sins thou wilt
apostatize from the order, and wilt die out
of the order; and over and above this, God
has revealed to me that thou wilt be
damned." Hearing this, Brother Elias
thus replied : "My reverend father, I beg
thee for the love of Jesus Christ, that thou
shun me not for this, nor spurn me from
thee, but as a good shepherd, after the
example of Christ, bring back and receive
the sheep that would perish without thine
aid. And pray God for me that, if it be
possible, He may revoke the sentence of
my damnation; because it is written that
God will change His sentence, if the sinner
amend him of his sins ; and I have so great
faith in thy prayers that if I were in the
midst of hell, and thou didst pray God for
me, I should feel some refreshment. Therefore again I beseech thee, recommend me,
sinner as I am, to God, who came to save
sinners, that He would receive me to His
mercy." And this Brother Elias said with
great devotion and with tears ; therefore
St Francis, as a compassionate father, promised to pray to God for him, and he did so.
And as he prayed most devoutly for him,
he understood by revelation that God had
heard his prayer so far as to revoke the
sentence of damnation against Brother
Elias, so that at the last his soul should not
be damned; but that still of a surety he
would leave the order, and out of the order
he would die ; and so it came to pass. For

Frederick, the king of Sicily, having rebelled against the Church, and being excommunicated by the pope—he and all who had counselled him and aided him—the said Brother Elias, who was reputed one of the most learned men in the world, being asked by this King Frederick, went over to him, and rebelled against the Church, and apostatized from the order ; for which cause he was excommunicated by the pope, and deprived of the habit of St Francis.

And being thus excommunicated and grievously sick, one of his brethren, a lay brother who had remained in the order and was a man of good and virtuous life, hearing of his sickness went to visit him, and after some other words said to him : " My most beloved brother, it grieves me sore that thou shouldst be excommunicated, and cast out of thine order, and that thou shouldst die thus ; but if thou seest way or means by which I could deliver thee from this peril, willingly would I take for thee any pains." And Brother Elias answered : " My brother, I see no other way unless thou go to the pope, and beg for the love of God and of St Francis his servant, through whose teaching I abandoned the world, that he would absolve me from his excommunication and restore to me the habit of religion." And his brother said that he would willingly take such pains upon himself for his salvation.

And departing from him, he went on

foot to the Holy Father, humbly praying
him that he would do grace to his brother,
for the love of Christ and St Francis his
servant. And as it pleased God, the pope
consented that he should return and, if he
found Brother Elias alive, should absolve
him in his name from the sentence of
excommunication, and restore to him the
habit. Therefore he departed joyfully, and
with great haste returned to Brother Elias,
and found him alive but almost at the point
of death, and absolved him from his excommunication. And Brother Elias, having put
on the habit again, departed this life, and
his soul was saved by the merits of St
Francis and by his prayer, in which Brother
Elias had placed such great hope.

XXXVIII—Of the wonderful Discourse which St Antony of Padua made in the Consistory

THAT wonderful vessel of the Holy Spirit,
St Antony of Padua, one of the chosen
disciples and companions of St Francis,
whom the latter called his vicar, was
preaching once before the pope and
the cardinals in the consistory. And there
were present men of divers nations—Greeks,
Latins, French, Germans, Slavonians, Eng-
lish, and others; and he was so inflamed
by the Holy Spirit, and explained the word
of God so devoutly, so sweetly, so clearly,
and in a manner so efficacious and so
learned, that all those who were in the con-

sistory, though they spoke different languages, understood what he said as perfectly as if he had spoken the language of each. And they were all full of wonder, for it seemed to them as if the miracle of the apostles at the time of Pentecost had been renewed, when the Holy Spirit taught them to speak all languages; and they said among themselves, " Does not he that preaches come from Spain? How is it, then, that we each hear in his words our own tongue spoken?" And the pope, as much surprised as the others, considering the deep meaning of his words, exclaimed, " In truth this man is the ark of the Testament, and the treasure of the Holy Scriptures."

XXXIX—Of the Miracle which God performed when St Antony preached to the Fishes.

CHRIST the blessed was pleased to show forth the great sanctity of His most faithful servant St Antony, and how men ought devoutly to listen to his preaching, by means of creatures without reason. On one occasion, amongst others, He made use of fishes to reprove the folly of faithless heretics, just as we read in the Old Testament how, in ancient times, He reproved the ignorance of Balaam by the mouth of an ass.

St Antony, being at one time at Rimini, where there were a great number of heretics, and wishing to lead them by the light of faith into the way of truth, preached to them

for several days, and reasoned with them
on the faith of Christ and on the Holy
Scriptures. They not only resisted his
words, but were hardened and obstinate,
and refused to listen to him. At last St
Antony, inspired by God, went down to
the sea-shore, where the river runs into the
sea, and, having placed himself on a bank
between the river and the sea, he began to
speak to the fishes as if the Lord had sent
him to preach to them, and said, " Listen
to the word of God, O you fishes of the sea
and river, as the faithless heretics refuse to
do so."

No sooner had he spoken these words
than suddenly a great multitude of fishes,
both small and great, approached the bank
on which he stood, and never before had so
many been seen in the sea or in the river;
all kept their heads out of the water, and
seemed to be attentively looking on St
Antony's face; all were ranged in perfect
order and most peacefully, the smaller ones
in front near the bank, after them came
those a little bigger, and last of all, where
the water was deeper, the large ones.

When they had placed themselves in
this order, St Antony began to preach
to them most solemnly, saying: " My
brothers the fishes, you are bound as
much as it is in your power to return thanks
to your Creator, who has given you such a
noble element for your dwelling; for you
have at your choice sweet water and salt

water; you have many places of refuge
from the tempest; you have likewise a pure
and transparent element for your nourishment. God, your bountiful and kind Creator,
when He made you, ordered you to increase
and multiply, and gave you His blessing.
In the universal deluge all other creatures
perished; you alone did God preserve from
all harm. He has given you fins to enable
you to go where you will. To you was it
granted, according to the commandment of
God, to keep the prophet Jonas, and after
three days to throw him safe and sound on
dry land. You it was who gave the tribute-
money to our Saviour Jesus Christ when,
through His poverty, He had nothing to
pay. By a singular mystery you were the
nourishment of the eternal King, Jesus
Christ, before and after His Resurrection.
Because of all these things you are bound
to praise and bless the Lord who has given
you so many and so much greater blessings
than to other creatures."

At these words the fishes began to open
their mouths and bow their heads, and
endeavoured, as much as was in their power,
to express their reverence and show forth
their praise. St Antony, seeing the reverence of the fishes towards their Creator,
rejoiced greatly in spirit, and said with
a loud voice: " Blessed be eternal God, for
the fishes of the sea honour Him more than
men without faith, and animals without
reason listen to His word with greater

attention than sinful heretics." And whilst
St Antony was preaching the number of the
fishes increased, and none of them left the
place he had chosen.

And the people of the city, hearing of
the miracle, made haste to go and witness
it. With them came the heretics of whom
we have spoken above, who, seeing such a
wonderful and manifest miracle, were
touched in their hearts, and all threw themselves at the feet of St Antony to hear his
words. The saint then began to expound
to them the Catholic faith. He preached so
eloquently that all those heretics were converted and returned to the true faith of
Christ ; the faithful were filled with joy and
greatly comforted and strengthened in the
faith. After this St Antony sent away the
fishes with the blessing of God ; and they
all departed rejoicing as they went, and the
people returned to the city. St Antony remained at Rimini for several days, preaching and reaping much spiritual fruit in the
souls of his hearers.

XL—How the venerable Brother Simon delivered a Brother from a great temptation

ABOUT the beginning of the order and
during the lifetime of St Francis, a young
man from Assisi, whose name was Simon,
took the habit ; and the Lord adorned him
with such graces and such elevation of
mind that all his life he was a mirror of

sanctity, as I heard from those who had lived with him for a long time. He very seldom left his cell, and whenever he was in company with the brothers he always spoke of God. He had never learnt grammar, and yet he talked of divine things and of the love of Christ in a way so elevated and with such profound wisdom that his words seemed to be supernatural.

One evening he went into the wood with Brother James of La Massa to speak of God ; and they spent the whole night conversing sweetly on divine love. When morning dawned, they seemed to have been together but a few minutes, as was related to me by the aforesaid Brother James. And Brother Simon received the illuminations of the divine charity with such inward delight and sweetness of spirit that oftentimes, when he felt them coming, he laid himself down in his bed, because the tranquil sweetness of the Holy Spirit produced in him not only repose of spirit, but of the body also ; and in these divine visitations he was many a time rapt in God, and became altogether insensible to the things of the body.

Now once when he was thus rapt in God, insensible to the world and inwardly burning with divine love, without consciousness of external things through his bodily senses, a brother, wishing to prove if this were so and to see if he truly was as he seemed to be, went and took a live coal from the fire and placed it upon his naked foot. And

Brother Simon felt nothing, and it made no mark on his foot, although it remained there so long that it went out of itself. The said Brother Simon, when he placed himself at table, before taking food for the body both took and gave spiritual food, speaking of God.

Once by his fervent conversation he converted a young man of San Severino, who was an exceedingly vain and worldly youth of that time, of noble blood and very delicate of body. And Brother Simon, having received the young man into the order, put by his secular clothes, and kept them in his own charge; and he remained with Brother Simon to be instructed in the regular observance. But the devil, who busies himself to thwart all good, loaded him with ardent temptations and stings of the flesh which he could by no means resist; therefore he came to Brother Simon, and said: "Give me back my clothes which I wore in the world, for I can no longer resist this temptation." And Brother Simon, having great compassion for him, said: "Sit down a little, my son, with me;" and began to speak of God in such a manner that the temptation went away; and when the temptation returned and he asked again for his clothes, Brother Simon still banished it by talking of God.

And when this had happened several times, finally one night the said temptation assailed him so violently that for nothing in the world could he resist it; and he went to

Brother Simon to demand back his secular clothes, because that noways could he remain any longer. And Brother Simon, as he was wont to do, made him sit down beside him and spoke to him of God, till the youth leant his head on the bosom of Brother Simon weeping for grief and sadness of heart. Then Brother Simon, for the great compassion he had for him, lifted his eyes to heaven, and made supplication ; and praying to God with the greatest fervour for him, he was presently rapt in ecstasy, and his prayer was heard of God. And when he returned to himself the young man felt himself entirely freed from this temptation as though he had never experienced it.

Thus was the fire of temptation exchanged for the fire of the Holy Spirit, because it had approached to the burning coal, namely to Brother Simon who was inflamed with the love of God and his neighbour. So much so that once, when a malefactor had been taken who was to have both his eyes put out, the aforesaid youth, filled with compassion, went with haste to the governor, and in open council and with many tears and devout prayers, begged that they would put out one of his eyes, and one only of the malefactor's, so that he might not remain deprived of his sight. But the governor and the council, seeing the great charity of this brother, forgave both the one and the other.

Once, when Brother Simon was in the

wood in prayer, and feeling great consolation in his soul, a flock of crows began to annoy him with their cries; wherefore he commanded them in the name of Jesus to depart and return no more; and those birds forthwith departing, from that time forward were never seen or heard either there or in all the country round. And this miracle was known in all the province of Fermo in which that community dwelt.

XLI—Of the glorious miracle which God worked by the hands of some holy Brothers; and how St Michael appeared and spoke to one of them, and the Blessed Virgin Mary came to the other

THE province of the March of Ancona was formerly adorned, as the firmament with its stars, with saints and exemplary brothers who, like the stars of heaven, have illuminated and adorned the order of St Francis and the world with their example and their doctrine. Amongst the rest, there was first of all Brother Lucido Antico, who was truly resplendent with sanctity and burning with divine charity; whose glorious tongue, inspired by the Holy Spirit, brought forth marvellous fruit in preaching. Another was Brother Bentivoglio of San Severino, who was seen by Brother Masseo, lifted up in the air for a great space whilst he was in prayer in the wood; through which miracle the devout Brother Masseo, being at the time

K

parish priest, left his parish and became a Friar Minor, and of so great sanctity that he worked many miracles, both living and dead; and his body reposes at Murro.

The above-mentioned Brother Benti-voglio, whilst sojourning once alone at Trave Bonanti in order to take charge of and serve a certain leper, received commandment from his superior to depart thence and go unto another place which was about fifteen miles distant. And, not willing to abandon the leper, he took him with great fervour of charity, and placed him on his shoulders, and carried him, from the dawn till the rising of the sun, all the fifteen miles of the way, even to the place where he was sent which was called Monte Sancino; which journey, if he had been an eagle, he could not have flown in so short a time; and this divine miracle put the whole country round in amazement and admiration.

Another was Brother Peter of Monticello, who was seen by Brother Servodio of Urbino, then guardian of the old community-house of Ancona, raised bodily five or six cubits above the ground, as high as the feet of the crucifix of the church, before which he was in prayer. And this same Brother Peter, having fasted with great devotion during the forty days' fast of St Michael, on the last day of the fast, whilst at his prayers in the church, was overheard by a young brother (who was constantly hiding under the high altar in order to observe some token of his sanctity)

talking with St Michael the Archangel, and
the words they were saying were these. St
Michael said : "Brother Peter, thou hast
faithfully given thyself much pain for me, and
in many ways afflicted thy body; lo! I am
come to comfort thee, and therefore ask what
grace thou wilt and I will obtain it for thee
from God." Then Peter answered : "Most
holy prince of the heavenly host, and most
faithful promoter of the divine love, and pious
protector of souls, I beg of thee this grace—
even to obtain for me from God the pardon of
my sins." And St Michael replied : "Ask
some other favour, for this grace I will obtain
for thee most easily." And Brother Peter
not asking him anything further, the archangel concluded : "By the faith and devotion
thou hast towards me I will obtain for thee
this grace that thou hast asked, and many
others." And having ended their speaking,
which lasted for a great while, the archangel St Michael departed from him, and left
him consoled exceedingly.

In the lifetime of this Brother Peter there
lived also the holy Brother Conrad Offida,
who was in the same community-house at
Forano, in the province of Ancona. The said
Brother Conrad went one day into the wood
for the contemplation of God, and Brother
Peter secretly followed him to see what would
happen. And Brother Conrad began to be
absorbed in prayer, and most fervently with
great devotion besought the holy Virgin
Mother that she would obtain for him this

grace from her blessed Son, that he might feel a little of that sweetness which St Simeon felt on the day of the Purification when he held in his arms the blessed Saviour Jesus. And having thus made his prayer, the merciful Virgin Mary granted it; and behold there appeared the Queen of heaven with her blessed Son in her arms, surrounded by an exceeding great and clear light. And approaching Brother Conrad, she placed that Divine Son in his arms, who received Him with tenderest devotion, embracing and kissing Him and pressing Him to his breast, totally dissolved and melted away in the divine love and in unspeakable consolation. And Brother Peter likewise, who saw all these things from his concealment, felt his soul filled with the greatest sweetness and consolation.

And when the blessed Virgin Mary had departed from Brother Conrad, Brother Peter returned with haste to the house, in order not to be seen by him. But nevertheless, when Brother Conrad came in, all full of joy and mirth, Brother Peter said to him : " O what heavenly and great consolation hast thou had to-day ! " Then said Brother Conrad, " What is it thou sayest, Brother Peter ? and what dost thou know about what I have had ? " " Well do I know, well do I know," quoth Brother Peter, " how the Virgin Mother with her blessed Son has visited thee." Then Brother Conrad who being truly humble desired to keep the grace of God secret, prayed him

that he would tell it to no one; and such
was the great love thenceforth between
these two that they seemed to have one
heart and one soul between them in everything. And the same Brother Conrad once,
whilst in the community-house of Siruolo,
by his prayers freed a woman who was
possessed, praying for her the whole of one
night; and, after being seen by her mother
in the morning, he escaped in order that he
might not be found and honoured by the
people.

XLII—How Brother Conrad of Offida converted a young Brother, being importuned
by the other Brothers because of him: and
how the said youthful Brother dying, appeared to Brother Conrad entreating that
he would pray for him

THE said Brother Conrad of Offida, full of
holy zeal for evangelical poverty and the
rule of St Francis, was of so religious a
life and of so great merit before God, that
the blessed Lord Christ honoured him both
in his life and in his death with many miracles; amongst which it came to pass once,
that being come to the community-house
at Offida as a guest, the brothers prayed
him, for the love of God and of charity, to
admonish a young brother that was in the
house, who behaved so childishly and dis-
orderly that he disturbed both old and
young of the community in saying the

divine office and in the other regular
observances, and cared little or nothing
that he did so.

Therefore Brother Conrad, moved with
compassion for the man and by the prayers
of the brothers, took him apart one day,
and in the fervour of charity spoke to him
such efficacious and holy words of instruction that, by the operation of divine grace,
the youth was suddenly turned from a child
into an elder in manners, and became so
obedient and gentle and careful and devoted,
and afterwards so peaceful and serviceable
and so studious of all virtue that, as at first
all the family were disturbed by him, so
now all were contented and consoled by
him, and they loved him greatly.

It came to pass, as it pleased God, that
soon after his conversion the young man
died, at which the other brothers sorrowed
very much. And a little while after his
death, his soul appeared to Brother Conrad
as he was praying fervently before the altar
in the said convent, and saluted him
reverently as "Father;" and Brother
Conrad asked: "Who art thou?" And the
other said: "I am the soul of that young
brother who died this day." And Brother
Conrad said: "O my son, most beloved,
how is it with thee?" And he answered:
"By the grace of God and by your instructions, so far well inasmuch as I have escaped damnation, but indeed for my sins
which I had not time to purge sufficiently

I suffer the exceedingly great pains of purgatory; but I pray thee, father, that, as by thy pity thou didst succour me whilst I yet lived, so now it may please thee to help me in my pains saying for me some *Pater nosters*, because thy prayer is very acceptable in the sight of God."

Then Brother Conrad, consenting with benignity to his request, and having said for him once the *Pater noster* with the *Requiem æternam*, the soul cried: " O most beloved father, how well and how refreshed I feel myself! now, I pray thee, say it once again." And Brother Conrad said it; and when he had done so the soul said to him : " Holy father, when thou prayest for me I feel my pains lightened ; therefore I pray thee that thou cease not to pray for me." Then Brother Conrad, seeing that this soul was so much helped by his prayers, said for him a hundred *Pater nosters ;* and when he had done so, the soul said to him : " I return thee thanks, most dear father, in the name of God and of holy charity, because by thy prayers thou hast delivered me from all pains and I am going to the heavenly kingdom." And so saying the soul departed. Then Brother Conrad, to give comfort and joy to the other brothers, related to them in order the whole vision. And thus the soul of this youth went to paradise through the merits of Brother Conrad.

XLIII—How the Mother of Christ appeared to Brother Conrad with St John Evangelist, and told him which of them bore most pain in the Passion of Christ

AT the time when there dwelt together in the province of Ancona at the community-house of Farona Brother Conrad and the before-mentioned Brother Peter, who were two heavenly men and two shining stars in all that province, there was so great charity between them that they seemed to be one heart and one soul. And they bound themselves together to this compact: that every consolation which the mercy of God gave to either of them they would own it to each other in charity and reveal it the one to the other.

This compact being made between them, it came to pass one day that Brother Peter, being in prayer and thinking with the deepest devotion over the Passion of Christ and how the most blessed Mother of Christ and St John Evangelist, the most beloved disciple, and St Francis were depicted at the foot of the cross by mental grief crucified with Christ, there came to him the desire to know which of the three had the greatest grief in the Passion of Christ: whether the Mother who bore Him, or the disciple who had slept upon His breast, or St Francis who was crucified with the wounds of Christ. And as he continued in this devout reflection, there appeared to him the Virgin Mother with St John Evangelist and with

St Francis arrayed in the noblest vestures
of beatific glory; but St Francis appeared
arrayed in yet more beautiful vesture than
St John.

And as Peter stood amazed at this
vision, St John consoled him and said to
him : "Be not afraid, most beloved brother,
for we have come to console thee in thy
doubt. Know then that the Mother of
Christ and I, above all other creatures,
grieved over the Passion of Christ; but
after us St Francis had greater grief than
all others, and therefore thou seest him in
so much glory." And Brother Peter asked
him : "Most holy apostle of Christ, why
does the raiment of St Francis appear
more beautiful than thine?" And St John
answered : "The reason is this, because
whilst he was on earth he wore a viler
raiment on his back than I did." And
having said these words, St John gave
Brother Peter a glorious vesture which he
carried in his hand, and said to him :
"Take this vesture which I have brought
to give to thee." And as St John would
have arrayed him in it, Brother Peter,
stupefied, fell to the earth, and began to
cry : "Brother Conrad! Brother Conrad,
most beloved! run hither to me quickly;
come and see a marvellous thing." And as
he said these words the holy vision disappeared. Then Brother Conrad coming to
him, he told him these things in order; and
they returned thanks to God.

XLIV—Of the conversion and life and miracles
and death of the holy Brother John della
Penna

To Brother John della Penna, while yet a
child and a secular in the province of
the Marches, there appeared one night a
Child most fair and beautiful, who called
him, saying: "John, go to St Stephen's,
where one of the Friars Minor is preaching;
believe his doctrine and give heed to his
words because I have sent him; and this
done thou must make a long journey, and
then thou shalt come to me." Which hearing, he immediately arose, and felt a great
change within his soul.

And he went his way to St Stephen's,
and found a great multitude of men and
women who were gathered together to hear
the preaching. And he who was to preach
was a brother named Philip, who was one
of the first brothers who had come into the
Marches of Ancona, and they had as yet
but few houses in Ancona. Brother Philip
therefore stood up to preach, and preached
with the greatest fervour, not with words
of human wisdom but by the virtue of the
spirit of Christ announcing the kingdom
of life eternal.

And the sermon being ended, the aforesaid child went to him and said: "Father,
if it please thee to receive me into the order,
I would willingly do penance and serve our
Lord Jesus Christ." Then Brother Philip,

seeing a marvellous innocence and a ready
will to serve God in the child, said to him:
"Come to me on such a day at Ricanati,
and I will have thee received;" in which
place the provincial chapter was to be held.
Whereupon the child, being most pure of
heart, thought that this was the great
journey he was to make according to the
revelation he had had, and that then he
should go to paradise; and this therefore
he thought to do as soon as he was received
into the order. He went therefore and was
received; and when he saw that his thoughts
were not fulfilled then, and since the minister
in chapter had said that whoever should
wish to go into the province of Provence by
the merit of holy obedience he would willingly give him permission, there then came
to him a great desire to go, thinking in his
heart that this was the great journey which
he must make before he could go to paradise. But being ashamed to speak of it, at
last he confided all to Brother Philip, who
had caused him to be received into the
order, and begged him earnestly to obtain
for him this favour that he should go into
the province of Provence. Then Brother
Philip, seeing his purity and his holy intention, obtained for him this permission.
Whereupon Brother John with great joy set
off and went, having this belief that when
he had accomplished that journey he should
go to paradise.

But, as it pleased God, he remained in

that province twenty-five years in the same
expectation and desire, showing the greatest
honesty of life and example, growing always
in favour with God and with the people and
exceedingly beloved of the brothers and the
seculars. And as he was praying devoutly
one day, and weeping and lamenting because his desire was not fulfilled and his
pilgrimage of this life was too much pro-
longed, Christ the blessed appeared to him,
at the sight of whom his soul entirely
melted away. And He said to him : " Son,
Brother John, ask of Me what thou wilt."
And he answered : " My Lord, I know not
what to ask Thee but Thyself, for I desire
nothing besides ; but this only I pray Thee
that Thou pardon me all my sins and give
me this grace, to see Thee another time
when I shall have the greater need." And
Jesus said : " Thy prayer is granted." And
this said, he departed, and Brother John
remained full of consolation.

At last the brothers of the Marches,
hearing the fame of his sanctity, exerted
themselves so much with the general that
he sent him his obedience that he should
return to the Marches ; and having received this obedience he joyfully went on
his way, thinking that at the end of the
journey he should go to heaven, according
to the promise of Christ. But when he had
returned to the province of the Marches, he
lived there thirty years ; and he was not
recognized by any of his relatives, and

every day he waited for the mercy of God
that He would fulfil His promise to him.
And in this time he fulfilled the office of
guardian several times with great discretion; and God performed many miracles
through him. And amongst other gifts
which he had from God, he had the spirit of
prophecy.

Now once on a time, being abroad from
the house, one of his novices was assaulted
by the devil and so strongly tempted that,
consenting to the temptation, he deliberated
within himself to leave the order so soon as
Brother John should have returned from
without. All of which temptation and de-
liberation being made known to Brother
John by the spirit of prophecy, he returned
home immediately, and called to him the
said novice, and bade him confess himself.
But before he confessed, he related to him
in order all his temptation as God had revealed it to him, and concluded thus:
"Son, because thou hast waited for me
and wouldst not depart without my blessing, God has given thee this grace that
never shalt thou go out of this order, but
thou shalt die in the order and in the grace
of God." Then this novice was confirmed
in good will, and remaining in the order
became a holy brother. And all this was
related to me by Brother Ugolino.

The same Brother John, who was a man
of glad and peaceful soul, rarely would
speak, but was a man given to great devotion

and prayer; especially after matins he would never return to his cell, but remain in the church until daylight in prayer. And as he prayed thus one night after matins an angel of God appeared to him, and said to him: " Brother John, thy lifetime is accomplished in which thou hast waited so long; and therefore I announce to thee from God that thou mayest ask what grace thou wilt. And I announce to thee besides that thou mayest choose which thou wilt—one day in purgatory or seven days' pain on earth." And Brother John choosing rather seven days of pain in this world immediately sickened of various infirmities, so that he was oppressed with great fever and with gout in his hands and feet and with pains in his side and many other illnesses. But that which was worst of all to him was that a devil stood in front of him, holding in his hand a great scroll inscribed with all the sins he had ever done or thought; and said to him: " For these thy sins, which thou hast committed by thought, word or deed, thou art damned to the lowest depths of hell." And he could not remember any good that he had done either in the order or ever elsewhere, but thought for this to be damned, as the devil said to him. Therefore, when any asked him how he fared, he answered: " Ill, for I am damned."

The brothers, seeing this, sent for an old brother named Brother Matthew of Monte Rubbiano, who was a holy man and a great

friend of Brother John's; and the said
Brother Matthew came to him on the seventh
day of his tribulation, and saluted him, and
asked how it was with him ; and he answered
it was ill with him, because he was damned.
Then Brother Matthew said : " Dost thou
not remember that thou hast many times
confessed thyself to me, and that I entirely
absolved thee from all thy sins ? Dost thou
not remember also that thou hast ever served
God in this holy order for many years ?
Lastly dost thou not remember that the
mercy of God exceeds all the sins of the
world and that the blessed Christ our Saviour
paid an infinite price to redeem us ? And
therefore have good hope that of a certainty
thou shalt be saved." And as he said this,
because the term of his purgation was
accomplished, the temptation went, and consolation came. And with great joy Brother
John said to Brother Matthew : " Because
thou hast fatigued thyself, and the hour is
late, I pray thee go and rest thyself." And
Brother Matthew was not willing to leave
him, but finally, as he pressed him much, he
left him and went to lie down ; and Brother
John remained alone with the brother who
served him. And lo! Christ the blessed
came in glory and splendour and with an
exceeding sweetness of fragrance, according
as He had promised him to appear to him
another time when he should have the
greater need, and healed him perfectly of all
his infirmities.

Then Brother John with clasped hands thanked God that he had made so good an end of the great journey of this present miserable life in the arms of Christ, to whom he commended his soul, passing from this mortal life to the life eternal with Christ the blessed, whom he had for so long a time desired and waited to see. And the said Brother John rests in the Convent della Penna.

XLV—How Brother Pacificus, being in prayer, saw the soul of Brother Humilitas, his brother, going up to heaven

IN the aforesaid province of the Marches after the death of St Francis, there were two brothers in the order together; the one named Brother Humilitas and the other Brother Pacificus, and they were men of very great sanctity and perfection. One, namely Brother Humilitas, was placed in the community-house at Soffiano, and there also he died: and the other belonged to another community at some distance thence. As it pleased God, Brother Pacificus, being alone one day in prayer in a solitary place, was rapt in ecstasy, and saw the soul of his brother, Brother Humilitas, at the moment of its departure from the body go straight to heaven without any let or hindrance whatever.

And it came to pass that after many years Brother Pacificus, who still survived,

was placed in the community of the same
house at Soffiano where his brother had
died. At this time the brothers, at the request of the lords of Bruforte, moved from
their house into another; wherefore they
took away with them, amongst other things,
the relics of the holy brothers who had died
in this house. And coming to the sepulchre
of Brother Humilitas, his brother, Brother
Pacificus, gathered his bones and washed
them in good wine, and then wrapped them
in a white cloth; and with great reverence
and devotion he kissed them and wept over
them. At which the other brothers marvelled, and took some scandal that he, being
a man of such great sanctity, should from
mere human and worldly affection as it
seemed, thus weep for his brother, and show
more devotion to his remains than to those
of the other brothers, who had been of no
less sanctity than Brother Humilitas and
were worthy of equal reverence.

And Brother Pacificus, knowing the
untoward thoughts of the brothers, humbly
gave them the satisfaction they required,
and said to them: "My dearest brothers,
be not surprised if I have done more for the
bones of my own brother than for the others;
for, blessed be God! I was not moved thereto, as you believe, by human affection; but
I did it, because when my brother departed
this life, as I was praying in a deserted
place and at a distance from him, I saw his
soul ascend by a straight path to heaven;

L

and therefore I am certain that his bones
are sacred, and ought to be in paradise.
And if God had given me the same certainty
as to the other brothers, I would have done
the same reverence to their remains as to
his." Then the brothers, seeing his holy
and pious intention, were well edified, and
praised God, who has done such marvellous
things in his holy ones, the brethren.

XLVI—Of the holy Brother to whom the
    Mother of Christ appeared when he was
    sick, bringing him three boxes of electuary

IN the aforesaid house at Soffiano, there
was in former times a Friar Minor of so
great a sanctity and grace, that he appeared
totally transformed by divine grace, and
continually ravished in God. On one occasion, as this brother, who was notably gifted
with the grace of contemplation, was wholly
absorbed and lifted towards God, there came
to him birds of many different kinds, and
familiarly perched on his shoulders, and on
his head and on his arms and his hands,
and all sang together marvellously. He
loved to be alone, and rarely would speak
to anyone, but when he was asked about
any matter whatsoever, answered so graciously and with such wisdom that he seemed
rather to be an angel than a man, and
he was ever in prayer and contemplation ;
so that the brothers held him in great reverence. When this brother had finished the

course of his holy life according to the
divine decrees, he became sick unto death, so
that he could not take anything either to
eat or to drink; and besides this he would
not take any medicine for the body, but all
his trust was in the heavenly Physician,
Jesus Christ the blessed, and in His Blessed
Mother; and thus he merited by the divine
clemency to be mercifully visited and tended.

Being therefore in his bed, and prepar-
ing himself for death with all his heart and
devotion, there appeared to him the glorious
Virgin Mary, Mother of Christ, with a great.
multitude of angels and of holy virgins,
and with great splendour they approached
his bed. Then he, beholding her, took
great comfort and joy both of soul and body;
and began humbly to pray that she would
intercede with her beloved Son, that by His
merits He would release him from the
prison of this miserable flesh. And as he
persevered in this petition with many tears
the holy Virgin Mother answered, calling
him by his name, and said to him : " Doubt
nothing, son, for thy prayer is heard, and I
am come to comfort thee a little before that
thou depart from this life." There were
along with the Virgin Mother of Christ three
holy virgins that carried in their hands
three precious boxes filled with an electuary
of surpassing fragrance and sweetness.
Then the glorious Virgin took one of the
boxes, and opened it, and the whole house
was filled with sweet odours, and taking

thereof with a spoon she gave to him that was sick; and as soon as he had tasted it, he felt within himself such comfort and such sweetness that it seemed as though his soul could no longer remain within his body. Therefore he began to say : " No more, O most holy and blessed Virgin Mother, O blessed physician and saving refuge of mankind, no more; for I cannot sustain such sweetness ! " But the benign and compassionate Mother continued to give him of the electuary until the whole box was emptied.

Then having emptied the first box, the Blessed Virgin took the second, and put the spoon into it to give him of that also; at which he cried out, saying : " O most Blessed Mother of God, my soul is almost melted away with the exceeding sweetness of the first heavenly food; how then can I sustain the second? I beseech thee, most blessed above all saints and angels, that thou give me no more." But the glorious Virgin Mary answered : " Taste, my son, yet a little more of this second box." And when she had given him a little thereof, she said : " Now, my son, it is enough; be comforted, for soon I will return for thee and lead thee to the kingdom of my Son, which thou hast ever sought and desired." And having so said, she took leave of him, and departed, leaving him so fortified and consoled through the sweetness of this electuary that he remained living for several days, strong and

well and without requiring any bodily
nourishment. And after some days, while
speaking joyfully with the brothers, he
passed with gladness and delight from this
miserable life.

XLVII—How Brother James of La Massa saw in a vision all the Friars Minor in the world under the likeness of a tree

BROTHER JAMES of La Massa, to whom
God opened the door of His secrets and
gave the perfect knowledge and understand-
ing of the Holy Scriptures and of future
events, was endowed also with so great
sanctity that Brother Giles of Assisi and
Brother Lucidus and Brother Mark of
Montino and Brother Juniper said of him
that they knew of no one in this world so
much after God's own heart as he. I also
had a great desire to see him, because once
when I was asking Brother John, a companion of the above-mentioned Brother
Giles, to explain to me a certain matter in
the spiritual life he said to me: " If you
would be well informed in the spiritual walk
seek to obtain an interview with Brother
James of La Massa, because Brother Giles
himself desired to be informed by him,
and none can add aught to his words or
take aught from them, for his mind has
penetrated into the divine secrets, and
his words are the words of the Holy
Spirit, and there is not a man upon earth

with whom I myself desire so much to speak."

This Brother James, in the beginning of the ministry of Brother John of Parma, whilst praying one day, was ravished in God, and remained three days rapt in this ecstasy, all bodily sensation being suspended; and in such a state of insensibility that the brothers doubted if he were not dead. And while in this rapture it was revealed to him by God what should hereafter come to pass within our order; for which cause when I heard of it, I was the more desirous to hear him and to speak with him. And when it pleased God to give me the consolation of conversing with him, I entreated him thus: " If what I have heard of thee be true, I pray thee keep it not hidden from me. I have heard that when thou wast as one dead for three days, God revealed to thee among other things what should befall our order: this was reported to me by Brother Matthew, the minister of the Marches, to whom thou didst reveal it by holy obedience." Then Brother James, with great humility, acknowledged that what Brother Matthew said was the truth.

And that which Brother Matthew told me was as follows: I knew a brother, said he, to whom God has shown what shall hereafter befall our order; for Brother James of La Massa revealed to me that after many other things which God made known to him about the state of the Church militant,

he was shown also in vision a tree, great
and beautiful, the roots of which were all of
gold, and the fruits were men, and these men
were all Friars Minor.   The principal
branches were distinct, according to the
number of provinces in the order, and each
branch bore as many friars as there were
severally belonging to the province repre-
sented by that branch.   And thus he knew
the number of all the brothers belonging to
each province in the order, and the names
of them all, and the state and condition of
each, and their offices and dignities, and the
graces and also the faults of each one of
them.   And he saw Brother John on the
topmost branch in the midst of all the
others, and the ministers of all the provinces
were at the top of the surrounding branches.

And after all this he beheld Jesus Christ
seated on a great and shining throne, and
He called St Francis to Him, and gave him
a chalice full of the spirit of life; and He
sent him forth, saying: "Go, visit thy
brethren, and give them to drink of this
chalice of the spirit of life, because Satan
shall arise against them, and shall buffet
them, and several of them shall fall, and
shall not be able to recover themselves."
And He gave him two angels to accompany
him.   Then St Francis came, and offered
the chalice of life to all his brothers: he
began, offering it first to Brother John of
Parma, who, receiving it, drank it all
fervently and with haste; and immediately

he became all shining as the sun. And after him St Francis offered it to each of the other brothers; but few of them received it with due reverence and devotion, or drank the whole of it. Those who received it devoutly and drank it all, immediately became resplendent as the sun, and those who wasted it and did not receive it with devotion, became black or dark and deformed and horrible to behold ; whilst those who drank part, and in part wasted it, became partly shining and partly dark, and each more or less according to the measure of their drinking or wasting the cup. But more than all the others, the aforesaid Brother John shone resplendent, who had more perfectly drunk out the contents of the chalice of life, by which also he had looked more deeply into the abyss of the infinite Light of Divinity ; and thus he had foreseen the adversity and tempest which would arise against this tree, and toss and beat down its branches. Therefore he came down from the top of the branch where he was, and went down lower than all the branches even to the bottom of the tree itself, where he remained hidden and in a thoughtful mood.

And behold a brother, who had drunk a part of the chalice and wasted the rest, climbed up the branch to the place whence Brother John had descended. And when he was seated thereon, the nails on his hands became sharp-cutting pieces of iron as keen as razors ; whereupon he quitted the branch

whither he had climbed, and with great
haste and fury would have thrown himself
upon Brother John to injure him.   But
Brother John seeing him coming cried aloud
and commended himself to Christ, who sat
upon the throne; and at the voice of his
crying, Christ called unto Him St Francis,
and gave him a sharp flint-stone, and said
to him : " Go, and with this stone cut off the
nails of this brother with which he would
tear Brother John, so that he may not be
able to hurt him."   And St Francis went,
and did as Christ had commanded him.
And when he had so done, there came a
tempest of wind, and shook the tree so
violently that the brothers fell to the earth ;
and all those who had wasted the whole of
the chalice fell first, and they were carried
away by demons into dark and penal habitations.   But Brother John and the others
who had drunk all the chalice were trans-
lated by the angels to the habitations of light,
and of life eternal and beatific splendour.

And the aforesaid Brother James perceived and distinguished each one of them
clearly according to his name and condition
and dignity.   And so greatly did the wind
blow against the tree that at the last it fell,
and the wind carried it away.   And immediately the storm ceased there arose from the
roots of this tree, which were of gold, another
tree entirely of gold, producing golden
leaves and flowers and fruits.   Of this tree,
and how it grew up and took root down-

wards, and its beauty, its fragrance and its
virtue, it is better to keep silence than to say
more at this time.

XLVIII—How Jesus Christ appeared to Brother John of Alvernia

AMONGST the other wise and holy brothers
and sons of St Francis, who, as Solomon
says, are the glory of their father, there was
in our own time in the aforesaid province of
the Marches the venerable and holy Brother
John of Fermo, who, on account of the length
of time he had lived in the famous house of
Alvernia and because he passed away there
from this life, was afterwards known as
Brother John of Alvernia. The same was a
man of great and singular holiness of life.

This Brother John, being as yet only a
secular and a child, desired above all things
the life of penance which preserves the
purity of the soul and of the body; so that
even as a little child he began to wear the
iron heart and girdle on his flesh and to use
great abstinence. And especially whilst he
abode with the canons of St Peter of Fermo,
who lived in great splendour, he fled all
carnal delights, and macerated his body
with great rigidity of abstinence. But his
companions in that place, being averse from
this, took away from him his iron girdle,
and hindered him in many ways from fasting; so that he bethought him, being inspired
thereto by God, to leave the world with the

lovers of it and to cast himself entirely into the arms of Christ crucified, in the habit of the crucified St Francis : and so he did.

And being received into the order whilst still but a child and committed to the care of the master of novices, he grew so greatly in piety and in the spiritual life that each time he heard the said master speaking of God, his heart melted like wax approaching the fire. And with so much sweetness and grace was he enkindled by the divine love that he could not contain himself, abiding in one place, but arose, and, as one inebriated with the spirit of God, ran to and fro about the garden or the wood or the church, according as the fire and impulses of the Holy Spirit led him. And thus in the process of time divine grace caused this angelic soul to grow continually from one degree of virtue to another, and in heavenly gifts and divine elevation and ecstasies ; so that his mind was lifted up—now to the splendours of the cherubim, now to the ardour of the seraphim, now to the joys of the blessed, and even to the ecstatic and loving embraces of Jesus Christ. And especially on one occasion above others, the flame of divine love so enkindled his heart that for three years after, during which it continued to remain with him, he received unceasingly the most marvellous consolations and divine visitations, and was constantly ravished in God ; and, in brief, during the whole time appeared to be all on fire and glowing with the love of Christ; and this took place in the holy Mount of Alvernia.

But because God has a singular care of His children, giving them variously at one time consolations, at another tribulations, now prosperity, now adversity, according as He sees that they have need to be maintained in humility, or else to increase in them the desire of heavenly things, it pleased the Divine Goodness, at the end of three years, to take away from the said Brother John the glow and fire of the divine love, and to deprive him of all spiritual consolation. And thus Brother John, being left without the light and love of God, was altogether disconsolate and afflicted : for which cause, in the anguish of his heart, he now went to and fro in the wood, seeking to recall with his voice and with tears and sighs the beloved Spouse of his soul, who had departed and hidden Himself from him, and without whose presence his soul found no solace or repose. But nowhere and in no way could he find his sweet Jesus, nor return to that spiritual sweetness which he had tasted in the love of Christ aforetime. And this tribulation lasted many days, during which he persevered in continual weeping and sighing to entreat of God to restore to him one day, of His pity, the beloved Spouse of his soul.

At last, when it had pleased God sufficiently to prove his patience and increase his desire, as Brother John was going as aforesaid through the wood burdened and af-

flicted, he sat down, overcome with weari-
ness, at the foot of a beech-tree, and thus
remained with his face all bathed in tears
looking up to heaven; and behold, suddenly
Jesus Christ appeared to him in the path
by which he himself had come, and stood
close by but without speaking a word.
Then Brother John, seeing and knowing
that it was the Lord, immediately cast himself at His feet, and with many tears most
humbly besought Him, saying: "Help me,
O my Lord, who without Thee, most sweet
Saviour, am in darkness and mourning;
without Thee, O most gentle Lamb of God,
I am in anguish and in pain and fear; without Thee, O Son of God Most High, I remain in shame and confusion; without Thee
I am blind and deprived of all good, for
Thou, Lord Jesus, art the true Light of our
souls; without Thee I am lost and damned
for ever, because Thou art the Life of our
souls and Life of life; without Thee I am
barren and withered, because Thou art the
fountain of grace and of all good gifts; without Thee I am altogether desolate, because
Thou art Jesus our Redemption, our love
and our desire, the Bread of consolation
and Wine that rejoices the hearts of the
angels and of all the saints. Enlighten
me, most gracious Master and most tender
Shepherd, for I am Thy little sheep, although unworthy so to be." But because
the desire of His saints, when God delays to
answer it, increases in them a greater love

and a greater merit, Christ the blessed departed without granting his prayer and without answering him a word by the same path
by which He came.

Then Brother John arose and ran after
Him, and again threw himself at His feet
and with holy importunity held Him back,
and with most fervent tears said to Him:
"O most sweet Lord Jesus Christ, have
pity on my tribulation; hear me through
the multitude of Thy mercies and by the
truth of Thy salvation, and restore to
me the joy of Thy countenance and look in
pity on me, because the whole earth is full
of Thy mercy." And yet again Christ departed, and neither spoke to him nor gave
him any consolation; but did with him as a
mother with her child, who, to make it the
more desire the breast, lets it follow her
crying, that it may take it the more willingly. Thus Brother John also followed
Christ with yet greater fervour and desire;
and when he was come to Him, Christ the
blessed turned and looked upon him with a
serene and gracious countenance, and taking
him in His most holy and merciful arms He
embraced him most tenderly. And as He
thus opened His arms, Brother John saw
issuing from the most Sacred Heart of the
Saviour rays of resplendent light which
illumined the whole wood and himself also
in body and soul. Then Brother John knelt
down at His feet, and the blessed Jesus, as
to a second Magdalene, graciously gave

him His foot to kiss; and Brother John,
holding it with all reverence, bathed it with
so many tears that he appeared indeed
another Magdalene, and said fervently: "I
beseech Thee, my Lord, that Thou look not
upon my sins, but by Thy most holy Passion
and by the sprinkling of Thy most precious
Blood revive my soul in the grace of Thy
love, seeing that this is the commandment
that Thou hast given us, that we should
love Thee with all our heart and with all
our affection; which commandment none
can keep without Thy help. Help me then,
O most beloved Son of God, that according
to Thy commandment I may love Thee with
all my heart and with all my strength."

And as Brother John prayed thus at the
feet of Christ, his prayer was heard, and he
received from Him the first grace, namely
the flame of divine love, and felt himself
entirely consoled and renewed. And knowing within himself that the gift of divine
grace was restored to him, he began to give
thanks to the blessed Christ and devoutly to
kiss his feet. And raising himself to see
Christ face to face, Jesus Christ held out to
him His most holy hands to kiss; and
when Brother John had kissed them, he
came nearer and leant on the breast of
Jesus and kissed it, and embraced Him;
and Christ also kissed and embraced him.
And whilst He did so, Brother John perceived so divine a fragrance that if all sweet
and fragrant odours of the world had been

united in one, they would have seemed but
a stink in comparison with that odour; and
thereby Brother John was ravished and consoled and inwardly illuminated, and he retained this sweet fragrance in his soul many
months.

And from that time forward his lips,
which had drunk from the fountain of divine
wisdom at the Sacred Heart of Jesus, uttered marvellous and celestial words, which
moved all hearts, and brought forth great
spiritual fruit in those that heard. And in
that path in the woods where the blessed
feet of Christ had stood, and for a good
distance around, Brother John always perceived the same fragrance and saw the same
resplendent light when he passed that way
for long after. And returning to himself
from his ecstasy, and the bodily presence of
Christ having vanished, his soul remained
so inwardly illumined from the depths of
His divinity that although he was a man
unlearned in human knowledge, nevertheless he marvellously solved and explained
the highest and most subtle questions as to
the Blessed Trinity and the most profound
mysteries of the Holy Scriptures. And
often afterwards he spoke before the pope
and the cardinals, and to the king and his
barons and the masters and doctors, and all
were astonished at the sublime words he
spoke and the profound judgments he gave
to them.

XLIX—How Brother John of Alvernia, as he
said Mass on All Souls Day, saw many
Souls delivered from Purgatory

As Brother John was once saying Mass on
the day after All Saints for the souls of all
the dead, as the Church has ordered, he
offered the most august Sacrifice—which for
its efficacy the holy souls desire more than
all other benefits whatever that can be con-
ferred upon them—with such fervent devotion and effectual charity that he seemed as
though entirely dissolved with the sweetness of his compassion and fraternal love.
And thus as he devoutly elevated the Body
of Christ and offered it to God the Father,
and prayed that, for the love of His blessed
Son, Jesus Christ, who hung upon the cross
for the redemption of our souls, it would
please Him to deliver from the pains of
purgatory the souls He had created and re-
deemed ; immediately he beheld an innumerable multitude of souls ascend out of
purgatory like sparks of fire out of a burning furnace, and he saw them go up into
heaven through the merits of the Passion of
Christ, which every day is offered for the
living and the dead in this most holy
Sacrifice, worthy to be adored through
all eternity.

L—Of Brother James of Fallerone, and how
   after his death he appeared to Brother
   John of Alvernia

BROTHER JAMES of Fallerone, a man of
great sanctity of life, was dangerously ill
once at the community of Moliano, which
was in the province of Fermo ; and Brother
John of Alvernia, who loved him as a dear
father, hearing of it betook himself to
prayer, earnestly entreating God in his
heart to restore him to bodily health if it
was for the good of his soul. And as he
prayed thus fervently, he was ravished in
ecstasy, and saw in the air above his cell,
which was in the wood, a great army of
saints and angels shining with such splendour that all the country round was illuminated by it ; and in the midst of the angels
he saw him for whom he prayed, Brother
James who was sick, arrayed in white and
shining garments. He saw also amongst
them the blessed father St Francis,
adorned with the sacred stigmas of Christ
and with great glory. Besides these he recognized the holy Brother Lucidus and
Brother Matthew of Monte Rubbiano, and
many other brothers whom he had never
seen or known in this life.

And as he looked with joy on this blessed
multitude of saints, it was revealed to him
that his brother who was sick should die in
this illness, and that for certain his soul should
be saved ; but that he should not enter para-

dise immediately on his death, because it behoved him first to be purified a little while in
purgatory. This revelation gave Brother
John such consolation that, for joy of the salvation of his brother's soul, he thought nothing more of the death of his body; but with
the greatest inward sweetness he called him
in spirit, saying: " Brother James, my sweet
father; Brother James, my beloved brother;
Brother James, most faithful servant and
friend of God; Brother James, companion of
the angels and fellow-citizen of the saints!"

And in the joy of this certainty he returned
to himself, and immediately he departed from
thence, and went to visit the said Brother
James at Moliano; and found him so weighed
down with sickness that hardly could he
speak. Then he announced to him his approaching death and the salvation and glory
of his soul, according to the certainty which
had been given him by the divine revelation,
which Brother James received with a joyful
heart and countenance so that he laughed for
mirth and gladness of his soul, thanking him
for the good tidings he had brought and devoutly commending himself to his prayers.
Then Brother John besought him earnestly
that he would return after his death and tell
him of his state, and this he promised to do if
it should please God. And having thus
spoken, and the hour of his departure being
near, Brother James began devoutly to recite
the verse of the Psalm : *In pace in idipsum
dormiam et requiescam;* which is to say, " I

will sleep in peace and rest in the life eternal ; " and having said these words with a bright and joyful countenance he passed away from this life.

And after his burial Brother John returned to the house at Massa, and waited for the promise of Brother James that he would return to him on the day he had said. But on the said day, as he was praying, Christ appeared to him with a great company of angels and saints, and Brother James was not among them ; at which Brother John greatly marvelling recommended him fervently to Christ our Lord. The following day, as Brother John was praying in the wood, Brother James appeared to him accompanied by angels all shining and glorious ; and Brother John said to him : " O father most beloved, wherefore didst thou not come to me on the day promised ? " And Brother John answered : " Because I had need of some purgation ; but in the same hour when Christ appeared to thee and thou didst commend me to Him, He heard thee, and delivered me from all pains. And immediately I appeared to Brother James of La Massa, that holy lay-brother who, as he served the Mass, beheld the sacred Host when the priest elevated it changed and transformed into the form of a fair and lovely Child ; to whom I said : ' Behold I go with this Child to the kingdom of eternal life, without whom none can enter there.' " And having said these words Brother James disappeared, and went up to heaven with all the blessed company of the angels ; and Brother John remained much consoled. Brother James of Fallerone died on the vigil of St James the Apostle in the month of July, in the above mentioned community-house of Moliano, where, after his death, many miracles were wrought through his merits by the Divine Goodness. ❦

LI—Of the vision of Brother John of Alvernia, whereby he understood all the order of the Holy Trinity

THIS Brother John of Alvernia, because he had perfectly stifled all worldly and temporal delights and consolations, and had placed all his delight and all his hope in God, received from the Divine Goodness marvellous consolations and revelations, especially on the feasts of our Blessed Lord. Now once, when the feast of the Nativity of Christ was approaching—when he confidently expected to receive special consolations from God, in the sweet humility of Jesus—the Holy Spirit put into his heart such an excessive and fervent love of the charity of Christ, which caused Him to humble Himself so far as to take upon Him our humanity, that it seemed to him as though in very deed his soul was being drawn from his body, and was burning like unto a furnace. And not being able to sustain this inward fire, he was in anguish, and as one wholly dissolved and melted away he cried out with a loud voice ; and he could not restrain himself from crying out because of the impetuosity of the Holy Spirit and the excessive fervour of his love. And in the same hour as there came to him this immeasurable fervour, there came to him also so strong and certain a hope of salvation that for nothing in the world could he believe that, had he died then, he should have had to pass through the pains of purgatory.

And this ardent love lasted over six months, although its excessive fervour was not continual but came to him at certain hours of the day. And during this time he received marvellous visitations and consolations from God, and at divers times he was rapt in ecstasy, as was seen by that brother who first wrote of these things. Amongst other such times, one night he was so raised up and ravished in God that he saw Him as the Creator of all things, and all created things in Him, both celestial and terrestrial and all their several perfections and grades and distinct orders. And then also he clearly perceived how all created things are present to their Creator, and how God is above and within and before and behind all His creatures. Afterwards he perceived God as One in Three Persons, and Three Persons in One only God, and the infinite charity which caused the Son of God to become incarnate in obedience to His Father. And finally, in the vision, he perceived how that there is no other way by which the soul can go to God and have life eternal but through Christ the blessed, who is the Way, the Truth and the Life of the soul.

❧

LII—How Brother John of Alvernia, as he was saying Mass, fell down as one dead

To the same Brother John of Alvernia, in the same community-house of Moliano, there befel once the following miraculous circumstance, as was related by the brothers who were present and saw it. On the first night after the octave of St Lawrence and within the octave of the Assumption of our Lady, having said matins in the church with the other brothers and feeling within himself the unction of divine grace coming upon him, he withdrew into the garden to contemplate the Passion of our Lord and to dispose himself to celebrate Mass, which it was his turn to sing that morning. And thus as he was meditating on the words of consecration of the Body of Christ, and considering the infinite charity of Christ therein, who would redeem us not only with His Precious Blood but by leaving us His adorable Body and Blood to be the food of our souls, he began to wax so full of fervour and tenderness in the love of his sweet Jesus that his soul could no longer contain itself for sweetness ; and he cried aloud and as though inebriated with the Holy Spirit, and ceased not to say, *Hoc est Corpus meum,* inasmuch as whilst saying these words it seemed to him that he saw Christ the blessed with His Virgin Mother and a multitude of angels,

and as he spoke to them he was inwardly illumined by the Holy Spirit as to the whole
height and depth of the mysteries of the most
august Sacrament.

And when the dawn was come, he entered the church under the same impression
and with the same fervour of spirit, and still
speaking the same words, not believing that
he was either heard or seen by anyone; but
there was a certain brother in the choir who
heard and saw all. And not being able to
contain himself by reason of the abundance
of the divine grace, he cried with a loud
voice, and continued to do so until it was
time to say the Mass, when he went and
prepared himself to go to the altar. And
when he had begun the Mass, the further he
proceeded the more there grew within him
the love of Christ and the fervour of devotion by which he received an ineffable impression of the Divinity, which he could
neither explain to himself nor express with
his tongue. Therefore, fearing that this
fervour and this impression would increase
so far that he should be obliged to discon-
tinue the Mass, he was in great perplexity,
and knew not which course to take, whether
to proceed with the Mass or to stand still
and wait.

But because on other occasions also the
same thing had befallen him, and our Lord
had so tempered this fervour that he had
been enabled to finish his Mass, and trusting
that it would be the same now as at other

times, he went on with the Mass, though with apprehension, and came as far as the preface of our Lady, when the divine illumination and the benign sweetness of the love of God began anew to grow within him with such force that, when he came to the *Qui pridie*, he could hardly sustain any longer such sweetness and delight. At last having come to the act of consecration, and having pronounced the first half of the words over the Host, namely *Hoc est enim*, by no means could he proceed any further, but continued only to repeat over again the same words. And the reason why he could go no further was because he saw and felt the presence of Christ amidst a multitude of angels, whose majesty he was unable to sustain; and he saw also that our Lord did not enter the Host, nor the Host become changed into the Body of Christ until he should be able to add the remaining half of the words, namely *Corpus meum*.

Wherefore as he stood thus in his anxiety and not proceeding any further, the guardian and the other brothers and many seculars besides, who were in the church hearing Mass, came round about the altar, and stood, looking on with astonishment and watching the actions of Brother John, and many of them were weeping through devotion. At last, after a great while, when it pleased God, Brother John added the words *Corpus meum*, with a loud voice; and immediately the form of the bread disappeared, and in the place of the Host there appeared Jesus Christ the blessed, incarnate and glorified, and made known to him the humility and the charity which He manifested in becoming incarnate of the Virgin Mary, and which He manifests every day in coming into the hands of the priest when he consecrates the Host: by which cause he was still more raised up in the sweetness of contemplation.

When he had elevated the Host and the consecrated Chalice, his soul was ravished, so that he became unconscious, and all sensation being suspended, his body fell backwards, and, if he had not been supported by the guardian who stood behind him, he would have fallen to the ground. Wherefore the brothers running to him, and the seculars also who were in the church, both men and women, carried him into the sacristy as one dead, for his body was cold, and his fingers were clenched so tightly that it was hardly possible to unclose or to move them. And he remained in this ecstasy as one half dead until the hour of terce. It was in the summer-time.

I, who was present also, desiring much to know what God had wrought in him, as soon as he had come to himself went to him, and prayed him, for the love of God, to tell me all that had taken place; and he, because he much confided in me, related the whole to me in order; and amongst other things he told me that whilst he was con-

sidering the Body and Blood of Jesus Christ
there present, his heart melted like wax in
a great heat, and it seemed to him as though
his flesh was without bones, so that scarcely
could he lift his arms or his hands to make
the sign of the cross on the Host or the
Chalice. And again he told me that before
he was made a priest it was revealed to him
by God that he should swoon in the Mass,
but because he had said many Masses
without this happening, he thought that the
revelation was not from God ; nevertheless
about fifty days before the Assumption of our
Lady, when this thing at last befel him, it was
again revealed to him by God that this
should be the case during the feast of the
Assumption; but that afterwards he had
no recollection of this vision, nor of the
revelation made to him by our Lord.

Of the Most Holy Stigmas of St Francis

🙰

I—The First Consideration

ST FRANCIS, being arrived at the age of forty-three years, in the year 1224 was inspired of God to leave the valley of Spoleto and to go into Romagna with Brother Leo, his companion. And as they went, they passed by the foot of the castle of Montefeltro, in which castle there was at that time assembled a great company and procession on account of one of the counts of Montefeltro being newly knighted. And St Francis hearing of this solemnity, and that there were there assembled many nobles and gentlemen from divers countries, said to Brother Leo: "Let us go to this festival; perhaps, with the help of God, we may produce good spiritual fruit there." Amongst the other nobles of the country who had come to this count was one, a great and wealthy gentleman of Tuscany, who was named Orlando da Chiusi of Casentino, who, for the wonders which he had heard concerning the sanctity of St Francis and the miracles worked by him, had a great veneration for him and a great desire to see him and to hear him preach. St Francis therefore, arriving at the castle, entered therein and went to the courtyard among the multitude of nobles and gentlemen assembled; and in fervour of spirit he mounted upon a parapet and began to preach, taking for the text of his sermon these words in the common language of the people: "So great is the good that I hope for that all pain delights me." And on this theme he discoursed by the dictation of the Holy Spirit so fervently and profoundly, citing the divers pains and sufferings of the holy apostles and holy martyrs and the severe penances of holy confessors and the manifold tribulations and temptations of holy virgins and other saints, that all the people stood with their eyes and their minds turned towards him, and listened as if an angel of God spoke.

Amongst the rest the aforesaid Orlando, touched to the heart by God through the marvellous preaching of St Francis, determined in his mind to confer with him after the sermon and take counsel on the affairs of his soul. Therefore, the sermon being ended, he took St Francis apart and said to him: "O father, I would converse with thee about the salvation of my soul." St Francis replied: "Most willingly; but go first and do honour to thy friends who have invited thee to the feast, and dine with them, and after the dinner we will talk as much as thou wilt." Orlando therefore went to dinner, and after dining he returned to St Francis, and conversed with him, and laid before him fully the state of his soul. And finally this Orlando said to St Francis: "I have in Tuscany a mountain called the Mount of Alvernia, a place most solitary, and as it would seem most holy, exactly suited to anyone who desired to do penance in a place remote from all men or to live a life of solitude ; and if it please thee I will willingly give it to thee and thy companions for the salvation of my soul." St Francis, hearing this generous offer of that which he greatly desired, rejoiced exceedingly, and praised and thanked God first and then Orlando, and said thus to him : " Orlando, when thou hast returned to thy house, I will send to thee some of my companions, and do thou show them this mountain, and if it appear to them suited for a place of penance and prayer, I will at that same hour accept thy charitable offer." And having said this, St Francis departed, and having completed his journey he returned to St Mary of the Angels; and likewise Orlando, after the festivities of the court were over, returned to his castle, which was called Chiusi and was a mile only from Alvernia.

St Francis therefore, having returned to St Mary of the Angels, sent two of his companions to Orlando, and when they were come to him he received them with very great joy and charity. And wishing to show them the mountain of Alvernia, he sent with them fifty armed men to defend them against the wild beasts of the forest ; and he himself accompanied the brothers, and they ascended the mountain, and diligently explored it. At last they came to a part of the mountain

most suited for devotion and for a place of
contemplation, where also there was a plain ;
and this spot they chose for their habitation
and that of St Francis. And, with the help
of the armed men who accompanied them,
they made cells with the branches of trees ;
and thus they accepted the gift in the name
of God, and took possession of the mountain
of Alvernia and of the habitation of the
brothers therein. And they departed and
returned to St Francis.

And when they were come to him, they
told him how and in what way they had taken
possession of a place on the mountain of
Alvernia specially suited to prayer and to
contemplation. Hearing these tidings St
Francis rejoiced greatly, and praised and
thanked God, and spoke to the brothers with
a joyful countenance, saying : " My sons, we
are approaching our lenten fast of St
Michael the Archangel ; I firmly believe that
it is the will of God we should pass this Lent
on the Mount Alvernia, on which by Divine
Providence a place has been prepared for us
that, to the honour and glory of God and His
glorious Virgin Mother Mary and of the holy
angels, we may, through penance, merit to
receive from Christ the consolation of con-
secrating this blessed mountain." And
having said this, St Francis took with him
Brother Masseo da Marignano of Assisi, who
was a man of great judgment and great
eloquence, and Brother Angelo Tancredi da
Rieti, a man of high and noble birth, who

had been a knight whilst in the world, and Brother Leo, a man of the greatest simplicity and purity, for which cause St Francis loved him much. And with these three brothers St Francis betook himself to prayer, recommending himself and the said three brothers to the prayers of those who remained, and set out with these three in the name of Jesus Christ crucified to go to Mount Alvernia.

And as they went, St Francis called to him one of his three companions, Brother Masseo, and said thus to him : " Thou, Brother Masseo, shalt be our guardian and our superior in this journey, whilst we are going and staying together, and we will observe one rule, that we may either be saying the office or speaking of God or keeping silence, and not thinking either of eating or drinking or sleeping; but when it is time to put up for the night, we will beg a little bread and remain and rest there where God shall provide for us." Then these three companions inclined their heads and made the sign of the cross and went on their way, and the first evening they came to a house of the friars, and lodged there. The second evening, because of the bad weather and because they could not reach any house belonging to the brothers nor any other house or castle, they took refuge from the weather in a deserted and ruined church and there laid down to rest. And when his companions slept, St Francis betook himself to prayer; and be-

hold, in the first watch of the night, there
came a great multitude of ferocious demons
with great noise and violence, and began
vehemently to attack and to torment him ;
one laid hold upon him on this side and one
on that; one pulled him up and another
pulled him down ; one threatened him with
one thing and one reproved him with another,
in order to distract him in his prayer ; but
they could not, because God was with him.

Therefore when St Francis had sufficiently borne the assaults of the demons, he
began to cry with a loud voice : " O damned
spirits, you can do nothing but what the
hand of God permits ; and in the name of
Almighty God I say to you, 'Do unto my body
whatever is permitted you by God ; know
that I will bear it willingly, because I have
no greater enemy than my body ; and therefore if you avenge me of my enemy you will
do me a great service.' "

Then the demons with the greatest impetuosity and fury took him, and began to
tear and to drag him about the church and
to make more disturbance and do him more
harm than at the first.   And St Francis
cried out and said : " My Lord Jesus Christ,
I give Thee thanks for so much honour and
charity which Thou dost unto me ; for this is
a sign of great love when the Lord punishes
well His servant for all his defects in this
world, for then he shall not be punished in
the next.   And I am ready to sustain joyfully all pains and all adversities which Thou,

N

my God, willest to send me for my sins."
Then the demons, confused and vanquished
by his constancy and patience, departed.

And St Francis in fervour of spirit went
out of the church, and went into a wood which
was near, and gave himself to prayer, and
with supplication and tears and beating of
his breast sought to find Jesus Christ, the
spouse and delight of his soul. And finding
Him at last in the secret depth of his soul,
he now spoke to Him reverently as his Lord;
now answered Him as his Judge; now besought Him as his Father; now conversed
with Him as with a friend.

On this night and in this wood his companions, who had come out after him and
remained to observe and to watch what he
did, saw and heard him with tears and supplications entreat the Divine Mercy for sinners. He was then seen and heard weeping with a loud voice over the Passion of
Christ as though he saw it before him with
his bodily eyes. In this selfsame night they
saw him praying with his arms stretched out
in the form of a cross, and for a great space
suspended and elevated above the earth, surrounded by a resplendent cloud. And thus,
in such holy exercises, he passed the whole
night without sleep.

And in the morning his companions,
knowing that through the fatigues of the
night which he had passed without sleep
St Francis was feeble in his body and might
take harm if he went on foot, they went to

a poor peasant and begged him, for the love
of God, to lend his ass for Brother Francis,
their father, who could not go on foot.
Hearing the name of Brother Francis, the
man said : " Are you of the brethren of that
Brother Francis of Assisi of whom so much
good is spoken ? " The brothers answered:
" Yes," and that it was indeed for him that
they had begged the ass. Then the good
man, with great devotion and solicitude, got
ready the ass and led him to St Francis,
and with great reverence helped him to
mount and to proceed on his journey;
and he went with them, walking behind
his ass.

And when they had gone some way, the
peasant said to St Francis : " Tell me, art
thou Brother Francis of Assisi ? " And St
Francis answered, " Yes." " Try then,"
said the peasant, "to be as good as all
think thee to be, because many have great
faith in thee; and therefore I admonish
thee to be nothing less than people hope of
thee." St Francis, hearing these words,
disdained not to be admonished by a
peasant, nor said within himself : " How
coarse and ignorant is he who admonishes!"
But he immediately dismounted and threw
himself on the ground, and knelt before the
man and kissed his feet; and thanked him
humbly for having condescended to admonish him so charitably. Then the
peasant, along with the companions of St
Francis, with great reverence lifted him

from the ground and replaced him on the
ass, and journeyed further.

And when they had gone about half
way up the mountain, the peasant began to
be very thirsty, because the heat was great
and the ascent fatiguing, and presently
began to cry behind St Francis, saying:
" Woe is me, how I pant for thirst ! if I do
not get something to drink I shall quickly
be choked." For which cause St Francis
descended from the ass and prostrated himself in prayer; and he remained on his
knees and with his hands lifted up to heaven
until he knew by revelation that God had
heard him. And St Francis said to the
peasant : " Run quickly to yonder stone,
and thou shalt find there living water, the
living water which Jesus Christ by His
mercy at this hour has caused to flow from
this stone." The man ran to the place
which St Francis had shown him, and found
a beautiful spring which sprang from the
hard rock by virtue of the prayer of St
Francis, and he drank copiously and was
comforted. And it was well seen that this
fountain was miraculously produced by God
at the prayer of St Francis, because neither
before nor since was there ever a fountain
of water in that place, nor any running
water anywhere near nor for a great space
around. This done, St Francis with his
companions and the peasant returned
thanks to God for the miracle He had
shown them, and journeyed further.

As they approached the foot of the rocks belonging to Alvernia; it pleased St Francis to rest awhile beneath the shade of the oak by the wayside, which is there to this day; and from under it he began to consider the lie of the country and of the place they were going to. And while he considered, there came a great multitude of birds from all parts, which, with singing and beating of their wings, all showed the greatest joy and gladness, and surrounded St Francis in such manner that some perched on his head, some on his shoulders, some on his arms and some on his legs, and some around his feet. His companions and the peasant seeing this and marvelling, St Francis, all joyful in his spirit, said to them : " I believe, most beloved brothers, that it pleases our Lord Jesus Christ that we should inhabit this solitary mountain, because so much joy is shown at our arrival by our little sisters and brothers, the birds." And saying thus, they arose and journeyed further, and at last came to the place which their companions had chosen beforehand.

II—The Second Consideration on the Holy Stigmas

ORLANDO, hearing that St Francis with three companions was about to ascend the mountain to take possession of it, was filled with joy. And the next day he set out with many people of his castle to visit them, taking with him bread and wine and other things needful for them. And when he arrived at the summit he found them all in prayer, and approaching he saluted them. Then St Francis, turning to him with the greatest benignity and joy, welcomed both him and his people, after which they sat down and conversed together.

And after they had talked awhile and St Francis had returned thanks to him for the holy mountain which he had given them, and for his coming to them, St Francis requested him also that he would build him a little cell at the foot of a beautiful beech-tree which was distant about a stone's throw from the place where the brothers were lodged, because it seemed to him a spot most apt and set apart for prayer. And Orlando immediately caused it to be built as St Francis had said. And this done, because the evening was now approaching and it was time to go, St Francis preached to them in a few words before they departed; and after he had preached and given them his blessing, Orlando took him and his companions aside and said to them: " My dearest brothers, I would not have you suffer any bodily want in this wild mountain by which you might be less able to attend to spiritual things ; and therefore I desire, and this I say to you once for all, that you will confidently send to my house for whatever you need ; and if you do otherwise it will give me very great pain." And

having said thus, he departed with his
people and returned to his castle.

Then St Francis made his companions
sit down, and instructed them as to what
manner of life they must lead, they and all
those who would lead religious and solitary
lives. And amongst other things, he ex-
horted them especially to the observance of
holy Poverty, saying: "Do not regard so
much the charitable offer of Orlando, as
that you in no ways offend against our lady
and mistress, holy Poverty. Know of a
surety that the more we shun Poverty the
more the world will shun us and the more
we shall suffer need; but if we closely embrace holy Poverty, the world will come
after us, and will provide for us abundantly.
God, who has called us into holy religion
for the salvation of the world, has made
this compact between us and the world,
that we are to give the world good example
and the world is to provide for our necessities. Let us therefore persevere in holy
Poverty, because this is the way of perfection and the earnest and pledge of eternal
riches." And after many holy and beautiful words and instructions on these matters
he concluded by saying : "This is the mode
of life which I impose on myself and on
you; and because I see myself to be near
the time of my death, I purpose to remain
in solitude and alone with God to weep
before Him over my sins; and Brother Leo,
when it seems good to him, can bring me a

little bread and water; but on no account
suffer any secular to come to me, but answer
for me to all that come." And having said
these words, he gave them his blessing, and
went his way to his cell by the beech-tree;
and his companions remained in the same
place with the firm resolution to observe
his commands.

And after some days, as St Francis was
standing by his cell considering the con-
formation of the mountain and marvelling
at the immense fissures and apertures in
the great rocks, it was revealed to him by
God while he prayed that these mighty
chasms had been miraculously opened in
the hour of the Passion of our Lord when,
as the evangelist relates, the rocks were
rent asunder. And it was the will of God
that this should more particularly take
place in this mountain of Alvernia, because
the Passion of our Lord Jesus Christ should
there be renewed in the soul of St Francis
by loving compassion, and in his body by
the sacred stigmas.

Having received this intimation, he immediately shut himself up in his cell, and
retired wholly into himself to await the
mystery that should be revealed. And from
this time forward he began, through the
unceasingness of his prayer, to taste more
frequently the sweetness of divine contemplation, through which oftentimes he was
rapt in God so that his companions saw him
raised bodily above the ground and com-

pletely ravished out of himself. In these contemplative raptures there were revealed to him by God not only things present and future, but even the secret thoughts and desires of the brothers, as Brother Leo, his companion, experienced within himself in those days.

This Brother Leo being assailed by the devil with a very great temptation, not of a carnal but of a spiritual nature, had a great desire to have something pious written by the hand of St Francis, and thought that if he had it the temptation would leave him either wholly or in part: but through shame and reverence he had not the courage to speak of this desire to St. Francis. But that which Brother Leo did not tell him was revealed to him by the Holy Spirit. Wherefore St Francis called him, and bade him fetch paper and pen and ink; and with his own hand inscribed the praise of Jesus Christ, signing it with the letter *Tau* * and gave it to him saying: "Take, most beloved brother, this paper, and keep it most diligently until thy death. May God bless thee, and keep thee against every temptation. And be not downcast because thou art tempted; for the more thou art assailed by temptation the more I repute thee the servant and friend of God and the more I love thee. Verily

---

* St Jerome, commenting on Ezechiel ix, says that in his time the letter *Tau*, which is the last letter of the Hebrew alphabet, was used in the Samaritan language to represent the cross of which it had the form.

I say to thee that none should esteem himself perfectly the friend of God except in so
far as he hath passed through many temptations and tribulations." And Brother Leo,
receiving this writing with all faith and devotion, immediately all the temptation departed from him ; and, returning to the place
where they lodged, he related to his companions with great joy the grace which he
had received from God through this writing
of St Francis ; and preserving and keeping
it diligently, the brothers afterwards worked
many miracles by means of it.

And from that hour the same brother
Leo began, with great purity of good intention, to observe slowly and to consider
the life of St Francis ; and by reason of his
purity he merited to see him again and
again ravished in God, and suspended above
the earth sometimes to a height of three,
sometimes to the height of four cubits, and
sometimes as high as the top of a beech-tree ;
and sometimes he saw him raised so high
above the earth, and surrounded with
such splendour that scarcely could he see
him at all. And what should this simple
brother do, when St Francis was elevated
from the ground only a little way, so that he
could reach him ? He went softly to him,
embraced his feet, and kissed them with
tears, saying : " My God, have mercy on me
a sinner, and through the merits of this
holy man give me to find grace with Thee."
And on one such occasion, standing thus

beneath the feet of St Francis when he was
raised so far above the earth that he could
not touch him, he saw a scroll written in
letters of gold descend from heaven and rest
on the breast of St Francis; and on the scroll
were written these words : *Here is the grace
of God;* and when he had read it he saw it
return into heaven.

By the gift of this grace of God which
was in him St Francis was not only ravished
in divine ecstatic contemplation, but also
on several occasions comforted by angelic
visitations.   Thus, as he was one day thinking of his death and of the state of his order
after his life should be ended, and saying :
"Lord, my God, what will become after my
death of this Thy poor little family, which of
Thy benign goodness Thou hast committed
to me a sinner ? who will comfort them ?
who will correct them ? who will pray to Thee
for them ?" and other such words, there
appeared to him an angel sent from God, and
comforted him, saying thus: "I declare to
thee on the part of God that the profession
of thine order shall never fail until the day of
judgment, and there shall never be so great
a sinner but that if he love thine order from
his heart he will find mercy with God, and
none who persecute thine order through
malice shall live a long life.   Moreover, no
wicked person within the order, if he amends
not his life, shall long remain in it.   And
therefore, grieve not thyself if thou see in
thine order certain brothers not good for

much who observe not the rule as they ought,
nor think that for this the order shall decline;
for there shall always be in it a great multitude who will follow perfectly the evangelical
life of the Gospel of Christ and the purity of
the rule, and then, immediately after the
death of the body, shall enter into life eternal
without passing through any purgatory;
others will follow it but not perfectly, and
these, before they enter paradise, shall suffer
purgatory, but the time of their purgation
shall be committed to thyself by God. But
as for those who do not observe the rules at
all, regard them not : for God Himself doth
not regard them." And the angel having
said these words departed, and St Francis
remained comforted and consoled.

After this, as the feast of the Assumption
of our Lady was approaching, St Francis
sought opportunity to lodge more solitarily
and secretly, that so he might the more
privately keep the forty days' fast of St
Michael, which begins with the feast of the
Assumption. And he called Brother Leo to
him, and spoke thus : " Go and stand in the
doorway of the oratory where the brothers
are lodged, and when I call thee return to
me." Brother Leo went therefore and stood
at the door ; and St Francis waited a little,
and called aloud. Then Brother Leo, hearing him call, returned to him ; and St Francis
said to him : " My son, let us seek another
more retired spot where thou canst not hear
me when I call." And seeking further they

found at some distance, on the southern side
of the mountain, a solitary spot exactly
suited to his desire; but it was impossible
to get to it because there lay an immense
rock with a yawning and fearful chasm in
front of it. But with great pains they laid
a piece of wood across it so as to form a
bridge, and got over.

Then St Francis sent for the other
brothers, and told them how it was his intention to pass the forty days' fast of St Michael
in this solitary spot; and he prayed them to
make him a little cell there, where no cry of
his could be heard by them. And when the
cell was made he said to them : " Go ye to
your place, and leave me alone, for I purpose,
with the help of God, to keep the fast un-
disturbed and without distraction of mind,
and therefore let not any of you come to me
nor suffer any one to come. But thou only,
Brother Leo, and once only in the day, come
to me with a little bread and water, and
once again in the night at the hour of matins;
and then come silently, and when thou art
at the end of the bridge thou shalt say :
Domine, labia mea aperies : if I answer thee
pass over, and come to the cell, but if I
answer thee not then depart quickly." And
St Francis said thus because several times
he had been so ravished in God that he had
neither heard anything nor felt any bodily
sensation. And having thus spoken he gave
them his blessing, and they returned to
their place.

And the feast of the Assumption being
now come, St Francis began to keep the
fast with very great abstinence and austerity,
macerating his body, and comforting his
spirit with fervent prayer, vigil and discipline; and in these his prayers he grew
continually from grace to grace, disposing
his soul to receive the divine mysteries and
the divine splendours, and his body to sustain the cruel assaults of the demons with
whom many a time he had bodily conflicts.
And amongst others it happened once during this fast that St Francis, coming one day
out of his cell and betaking himself fervently
to prayer in the hollow of a cleft rock from
whence a fearful precipice descended from
an immense height to the ground, the devil
suddenly appeared to him under a terrible
form with a very great tempest and tumult,
and struck him in order to thrust him down
the precipice. Then St Francis, having nowhere to fly and not being able to endure the
hideous aspect of the demon, turned quickly
back, and sought with hands and feet and
with all his body to cling to the rock, recommending himself to God and feeling about
with his hands for something to hold on to.
But as it pleased God, who never suffers His
servants to be tempted above what they are
able to bear, the rock to which he was cling-
ing immediately hollowed itself into the
shape of his body, and received him into
itself so that he sank into it as though it
had been melted wax, imprinting the form

of his hands and face on the rock : and thus,
by the help of God, he escaped from the devil.

But that which the evil spirit could not
do at that time to St Francis, he did a good
while after his death to one of his dear and
holy brothers, who was carrying some pieces
of wood to the same place in order to make
it possible to visit it without peril out of devotion to St Francis and the miracle which
had there taken place. One day the devil
pushed him with violence when he had a
large log on his head which he was going
to lay across the chasm, and caused him to
fall down with the log still upon his head.
But God, who had concealed and preserved
St Francis from falling, by his merits concealed and preserved the brother also from
the peril of his fall; for, as he fell, he commended himself with a loud voice and with
great devotion to St Francis, who immediately appeared to him and took him and
placed him gently down at the foot of the
rocks without his having sustained the least
shake or bruise. Now the brothers, who had
heard him cry out as he fell, believed that he
must be dead considering the great height
from which he had fallen and the sharpness
of the rocks beneath him ; and they took a
bier, and, with great sorrow and weeping,
came from the other side of the mountain
with intent to gather up the fragments of his
body and to bury them. And when they
had descended the mountain, the brother
who had fallen came to meet them with the

same log on his head with which he had
fallen and singing *Te Deum laudamus* with a
loud voice. And as they greatly marvelled,
he related to them in order all the manner
of his fall, and how St Francis had rescued
him from all peril. Then all the brothers
went with him to the spot, devoutly singing
the *Te Deum laudamus*, and praising and
thanking God and St Francis for the miracle
which had been performed for their brother.

Now in the aforesaid forty days' fast St
Francis, as has been already told, although
he sustained many attacks from the demons,
yet nevertheless received much consolation
from God not only through angelic visitations but through the birds of the wood.
For during all the time of the fast, a falcon,
which had built its nest close to the cell,
woke him every night a little before matins
with its note and with the beating of its
wings against the cell, and departed not
until he arose to say his matins; and when
St Francis happened to be more weary
than usual, or weak and infirm, the falcon,
like a discreet and compassionate person,
woke him later than usual. And for this
cause St Francis took great delight in this
bird, because by its great solicitude for him
it drove from him all idleness, constantly
inviting him to prayer; and besides this,
oftentimes by day it would sit familiarly
with him.

St Francis, being greatly weakened in
body through his great abstinence and the

assaults of the demons, and desiring to sustain his body by the spiritual nourishment of the soul, began to think upon the immeasurable glory and joy of the blessed in the life eternal, and to pray that God would grant him the favour of tasting a little of this joy. And as he thought thus within himself, suddenly there appeared to him an angel in great splendour, who had a viol in his left hand and in his right hand a bow; and whilst St Francis stood stupefied at the vision the angel drew the bow once across the viol, and immediately there was heard such sweet melody that his soul was inebriated with sweetness, and he lost all bodily sense; insomuch that, as he afterwards related to his companions, he thought that if the angel had drawn the bow a second time across the strings, his soul, through excessive sweetness, would have parted from his body.

III—The Third Consideration on the Holy Stigmas

IT came to pass, at the approach of the feast of the most holy Cross in the middle of September, that Brother Leo went one night to the usual place and at the same hour to say matins with St Francis. And calling from the top of the bridge, according to custom, *Domine labia mea aperies*, and St Francis not responding, Brother Leo did not go back as St Francis had commanded him, but with a good and holy intention

o

passed over the bridge, and went softly into
his cell, and not finding him there thought
he had gone to some place in the wood to
pray. Wherefore he went out again, and
by the light of the moon went softly search-
ing through the wood; and at last he heard
the voice of St Francis, and approaching
him he saw him on his knees in prayer with
his face and his hands raised to heaven, and
heard him say in fervour of spirit: "Who
art thou, O my most sweet God? and what
am I, most vile worm, and thy worthless
servant?" And these same words he
repeated continually, and said nothing
besides.

At which Brother Leo marvelling raised
his eyes looking up to heaven, and as he
looked he saw coming from heaven a torch
of fire, most resplendent and beautiful,
which descended and rested on the head of
St Francis; and from this flame he heard a
voice issue forth which spoke with St
Francis, but Brother Leo could not understand the words. Hearing this voice, and
judging himself unworthy to stay so near
the holy ground when this wonderful apparition was taking place, and fearing
besides to offend St Francis or to trouble
him in his contemplation if he should perceive his presence, he withdrew softly into
the background, and standing afar off
waited to see the end. And looking fixedly,
he saw St Francis extend his hands three
times to the flame; and finally, after a great

space of time, he saw the flame return to heaven. After this he departed securely and glad at heart at the vision he had seen, and returned towards his cell.

But as he went thus, secure in his own mind, St Francis perceived him by the rustling of the leaves under his feet, and commanded him to wait for him and not to move. Then Brother Leo obediently stood still and waited with such fear that, as he afterwards told his companions, at that moment he would rather the earth should swallow him up than wait for St Francis, as he thought he would be displeased with him; because he was wont with all diligence to guard himself against offending his father, lest for his fault St Francis should deprive him of his company.

Then St Francis coming to him, asked: "Who art thou?" And he, all trembling, replied: "I am Brother Leo, my father." And St Francis said to him: "Wherefore hast thou come here, Brother Little Sheep? have not I told thee not to come and observe me? Tell me by holy obedience if thou hast seen or heard aught?" Brother Leo answered: "Father, I heard thee say several times: 'Who art Thou, O my most sweet God? who am I, most vile worm, and Thy worthless servant?'" And then, kneeling down before St Francis, Brother Leo confessed the fault of disobedience which he had committed against his command, and implored his pardon with many tears. And

afterwards he prayed him earnestly to expound to him the words he had heard and
to declare to him those which he had not
understood.

Then St Francis, seeing that God had
revealed this to the humble Brother Leo,
and that He had indeed permitted him for
his simplicity and piety to hear and to see
so much, condescended to reveal and to explain to him that which he had asked,
saying: " Know, Brother Little Sheep of
Jesus Christ, that when I said these words
which thou heardest there was shown to me
in my soul two lights, one of the under-
standing of myself, the other the knowledge
of the Creator.   When I said: ' Who art
thou, O my most sweet God?' then I was
in that light of contemplation in which I
saw the depths of the infinity of the goodness and wisdom and power of God; and
when I said: ' What am I?' I was in that
light of contemplation in which I saw the
profound deplorableness of my own vileness
and misery; and then I said: ' Who art
Thou, Lord of infinite goodness and
wisdom, who dost deign to visit me who am
a vile and abominable worm?' and in that
flame which thou sawest was God, who
spoke to me in this manner as He spoke of
old to Moses.   And amongst other things
which He said to me He asked of me that
I should give Him three gifts; and I
answered Him: ' My Lord, I am all Thine;
Thou knowest that I have nought but my

tunic and my cord, and even these things
are Thine; what then can I offer and give
to Thy Majesty?' Then God said to me:
'Seek in thy bosom, and offer Me what thou
shalt find there.' I sought therefore therein and found a ball of gold, and I offered it
to God; and thus I did three times according as God three times commanded me;
and then I knelt down thrice and blessed
and thanked God, who had given me something to offer Him. And immediately it
was given me to understand that these
three offerings signified holy obedience,
uttermost poverty and resplendent chastity,
which God by His grace has given me to
observe so perfectly that in nothing my
conscience reproves me. And as thou didst
see me put my hand in my bosom and offer
to God these three virtues, signified by the
three balls of gold which God had placed
there, thus has God given me virtue in my
soul, that for all the benefits and all the
graces which His most holy goodness has
bestowed on me I should ever with my
heart and my mouth praise and magnify
Him. These are the words which thou
heardest when thou sawest me lift up my
hands three times. But take heed to thyself, Brother Little Sheep, that thou watch
me no more, and return to thy cell with the
blessing of God, and have a care for me;
because in a few days God will do such
great things on this mountain that all the
world will wonder; for He will do some new

thing which He has never yet done to any creature in this world."

And having said these words he had the book of the Gospel brought to him, because God had put it into his soul that after three times opening the book of the Gospel it should be shown to him what it would please God to do with him. And the book being brought to him, St Francis prostrated himself in prayer. His prayer being finished, he had the book opened three times by the hand of Brother Leo in the name of the most Holy Trinity; and as it pleased the Divine Providence in each of these three times, there always appeared the Passion of Christ. By this thing it was given him to understand that, as he had followed Christ in the acts of His life, so he must follow Him and be conformed to Him in His afflictions and sorrows and in His Passion, before he should pass out of this life. And from this time forward St Francis began to taste and to feel more abundantly the sweetness of divine contemplation and of the divine visitations, by one of which he had an immediate preparation for the impression of the most holy stigmas; and in this wise.

The day before the feast of the most holy Cross, in the middle of September, St Francis being secretly in prayer within his cell, an angel of God appeared to him, and said to him on the part of God: " I have come to comfort thee and to admonish thee

that thou prepare and dispose thyself
humbly and with all patience to receive
that which God shall give to thee and work
in thee." St Francis replied : " I am ready
to receive patiently everything that it
pleases my Lord to do unto me." And
when he had said thus, the angel departed.

The next day being come, namely the
feast of the most holy Cross, St Francis
prostrated himself betimes in prayer before
the opening of his cell, and inclined with
his face towards the east according to his
wont, praying thus : " O my Lord Jesus
Christ, I pray Thee to grant me two graces
before I die : the first, that in my lifetime
I may feel in my soul and in my body, so
far as is possible all the pain and grief
which Thou, O sweet Lord, didst feel in Thy
most bitter Passion ; the second, that I may
feel in my heart, as far as is possible, that
excessive love by which Thou, the Son of
God, wert impelled willingly to sustain so
great sufferings for sinners." And he remained a long time thus in prayer, trusting
that God would grant him what he asked,
and that, so far as it was possible for a mere
creature, it should be permitted to him to
feel these things as he had said.

Then, having received this promise, St
Francis began to contemplate with the
deepest devotion the Passion of Christ and
His infinite charity. And being inflamed
by this contemplation, on this same morning he saw coming from heaven a seraph

with six fiery and resplendent wings, and
approaching him with great speed, so that
he could discern him clearly and know
certainly that he had the form of a man
crucified, and that his wings were so disposed that two extended themselves above
his head, two stretched themselves in the act
of flight and two covered his whole body.
Seeing this St Francis was much afraid,
and filled at one and the same time with joy
and grief and admiration. He had the
greatest joy at seeing the gracious aspect
of Christ, who appeared to him so familiarly
and looked upon him so graciously; but on
the other hand, seeing Him nailed to the
cross, he had immeasurable grief and compassion. At the same time he marvelled
much at this stupendous and unwonted
vision, knowing well that the infirmity of
the Passion did not agree with the immor-
tality of the seraphic spirit. And being in
this amazement, it was revealed to him by
the seraphic spirit that by Divine Providence the vision was shown to him in this
form because God intended that, by the in-
flaming of his mind and not by corporal
martyrdom, he should be wholly transformed into the express similitude of Christ
crucified through this admirable apparition.

The whole mountain of Alvernia then
appeared burning with resplendent flame,
which shone forth and illuminated all the
mountain and the valleys around as though
the sun were risen upon the earth; so that

the shepherds, who were watching their
flocks in that country, seeing all the
mountain as it were on fire and so great
light around it, had the greatest fear, as
they afterwards related to the brothers,
affirming that this illumination remained
upon the mountain of Alvernia for the space
of an hour or more. In like manner, owing
to the splendour of this light, which shone
through the windows of the hostelries of the
country round, certain muleteers who were
going into Romagna rose with haste, believing that it came from the rising of the
sun, and saddled and loaded their beasts ;
and as they journeyed along they saw the
light cease and the natural sun rise.

After the said seraphic apparition, Christ,
who then appeared to him, spoke to St
Francis certain high and secret things which
he would not reveal during his lifetime to
anyone ; but after his life was ended he
revealed them, as will be shown further on ;
and these were his words : " Knowest thou
what I have done unto thee ? I have given
thee the stigmas which are the signs
of My Passion, because thou shalt be My
ambassador. And even as I on the day of
My death descended into Limbo and delivered all the souls I found there, by virtue
of My wounds, so also do I grant to thee
that every year on the anniversary of thy
death thou shalt go to purgatory, and all
the souls thou shalt find there of thy three
orders, namely of the Friars Minor, of the

sisters and virgins, and of the others also who shall have remained sincerely devoted to thee, thou shalt deliver by virtue of these thy stigmas, and shalt lead them into the glories of paradise, that so thou mayest be conformed to Me in thy death as thou hast been in thy life."

Then this wonderful vision disappeared after a great space of time and of secret converse, leaving in the heart of St Francis an excessive ardour and flame of divine love and in his flesh a marvellous image of and resemblance to the Passion of Christ. For in his hands and feet there immediately began to appear the marks of the nails in the same manner as he had seen them in the flesh of Jesus Christ crucified, who had appeared to him under the form of the seraph, so that his hands and feet appeared to be pierced through the middle with nails, the heads of which were in the palms of his hands and the soles of his feet; and the points came out again in the back of the hands and the feet, and were turned back and clinched in such manner that within the bend formed by the reversal of the points a finger could easily be placed as in a ring; and the heads of the nails were round and black. Similarly in his right side there was the appearance of a wound made by a lance, not healed but red and bleeding, which many times ran with blood from the holy heart of St Francis, and stained his tunic and his

nether garments. Whence his companions,
before they knew it from himself, perceiving
that he never uncovered his hands or his
feet and that he could not put the soles of
his feet to the ground, and afterwards finding his tunic and other garments stained
with blood when they washed them, understood with certainty that in his hands and
feet and also in his side he bore the exact
image and similitude of our Lord Jesus Christ
crucified. And whilst he exerted himself to
the uttermost to hide and to conceal those
sacred and glorious stigmas so clearly impressed in his flesh, and on the other hand
found that he could hardly conceal them
from his familiar companions, fearing to
publish the secrets of God, he was nevertheless in great doubt whether he ought to
reveal the seraphic vision and the impression of the most holy stigmas.

Finally, incited thereto by his conscience,
he called to him all his most familiar companions, and propounded to them his doubt
in general words and without explaining
to them the fact, asking their counsel.
Amongst these brothers there was one of
great sanctity named Brother Illuminato.
He, being truly illumined of God, understood that St Francis must have seen
something marvellous, and answered him :
" Brother Francis, know that not for thyself
alone but also for others God has shown
thee on several occasions His hidden mysteries ; and therefore thou hast reason to

fear lest, if thou keep concealed what God
has shown thee for the benefit of others,
thou shouldst be worthy of censure." Then
St Francis, moved by his words, with great
fear related to them all the mode and the
form of the aforesaid vision ; adding that
Christ, who had appeared to him, had
spoken to him certain things which he
would never tell so long as he lived. And
although those most holy wounds, inasmuch
as they had been impressed on him by
Christ Himself, gave the greatest joy to his
heart, nevertheless in his flesh and to his
bodily sensation they gave intolerable pain.
Whence, constrained by necessity, he chose
Brother Leo amongst all the others as the
most simple and the most pure, to whom he
revealed all, and he let him see and touch
those holy wounds, and bind them with
handkerchiefs to mitigate the pain and to
receive the blood which issued and dropped
from them ; which bandages, in time of
sickness, he let him change frequently even
every day, except from Friday evening to
Saturday morning; because during that time
in which our Lord Jesus Christ was crucified
for us, dead and buried, he would not allow
the pains of the Passion of Christ which he
bore in his body to be mitigated for him by
any human remedy or medicine. And it
happened several times when Brother Leo
was removing the bandages from the wounds,
that St Francis, through the pain which it
gave him to have them torn off, put his

hands on the breast of Brother Leo, who by
the touch of those holy hands felt such
sweetness of devotion in his heart that he
nearly fell to the ground. '

St Francis, having completed the fast of
St Michael the Archangel, soon after disposed himself by divine revelation to return
to St Mary of the Angels. Therefore he called
to him Brother Masseo and Brother Angelo,
and after many words of farewell and of holy
instruction he commended to them, with all
the earnestness he could, the care of that holy
mountain, saying that as for Brother Leo and
himself, it behoved them to return to St Mary
of the Angels. And having thus said, he
was accompanied by them a part of the way,
and blessed them all in the name of Jesus
crucified. And yielding to their prayers he
gave them his holy hands adorned with those
glorious and sacred stigmas to see and touch
and to kiss; and so leaving them comforted,
he departed from them and descended from
the holy mountain.

IV—The Fourth Consideration on the Holy Stigmas

WE have now to relate how St Francis, having
completed the forty days' fast in honour of
St Michael on the holy mountain of Alvernia,
descended the mount with Brother Leo and
with a devout peasant, on whose ass also he
rode because that for the nails in his feet
he could not well put them to the ground.

When he had come down, therefore, from the mountain—the fame of his sanctity having spread through the country, and the shepherds having declared how they had seen the whole mountain of Alvernia lit up and in flames, and that this must be the sign of some great miracle God had worked in him—as soon as the people of the country heard that he was passing, all of them made haste to see him, both men and women, great and small; and all of them with the greatest devotion and desire sought to touch and to kiss his hands. And not being able to escape the devotion of the people, although the palms of his hands were wrapped in bandages, he concealed them also beneath the sleeves of the habit, the more to hide the secrets of God, and only allowed his fingers to be seen and kissed. But for all his pains to hide the sacred mystery of the holy stigmas in order to fly the occasion of earthly glory, it pleased God, for His own glory, to show forth many miracles by virtue of them; and most especially during this journey from Alvernia to St Mary of the Angels, as well as many more afterwards in divers parts of the world, both during his life and after his glorious death, in order that by these clear and evident miracles the hidden and marvellous virtue of the most holy stigmas, and the excessive charity and mercy of Christ so wonderfully shown in his regard might be manifested to the world; and of these we will only relate the following.

One day, as he approached a village on

the confines of the district of Arezzo, a woman
came to meet him, shedding many tears and
carrying her son in her arms, who had suffered
from dropsy for eight years, ever since he was
four years of age, and whose body was so en-
larged that when he stood upright he could
not see his feet. And she set him down before St Francis, and besought him to entreat
God for him. Then St Francis first of all betook himself to prayer; and his prayer being
ended, he placed his holy hands on the body
of the child, and immediately the swelling
disappeared and he was perfectly healed.
And he restored him to his mother, who received him with the greatest joy, and led him
back to the house, returning thanks to God
and St Francis, and willingly showing her
little son, now restored to health, to all who
dwelt in that country and came to her house
to see him.

On the same day St Francis passed
through the borough of St Sepulchre; and as
he approached the castle, the inhabitants of
the town and of the country round went forth
to meet him, and many of them went before
him with branches of olive in their hands,
crying aloud : " Here is the saint ! Here is the
saint ! " And through the devotion of the
people and the desire that they had to touch
him, there was a great throng, and they
pressed upon him. But he, going his way
with his mind elevated and ravished in God
through contemplation, although the people
touched him and held him and pulled him,

passed on like one insensible, knowing
nothing of what was going on around him,
either what was said or done, never aware
that he was passing near the castle or
through that country. And when he had
passed through the town, and the people had
returned to their homes, he came to a leper-
house about a mile beyond the town. And
returning to himself as one coming back
from another world, the heavenly contemplative asked his companions: "When shall we
be getting near the town ?" Thus truly his
soul, fixed and ravished in the contemplation
of heavenly things, had no consciousness of
the things of earth, or of change of place, or
of time, or of those who went by. And this
was often the case, as his companions by
direct experience clearly perceived.

The same evening they arrived at the
community-house of Monte Casale, where
was a sick brother so cruelly and horribly
tormented by his illness that it seemed rather
as though it were some infliction and torment
of the devil than natural infirmity ; for often
he would fling himself down on the earth,
trembling violently and foaming at the
mouth; and sometimes there would come a
twitching of all the nerves of his body ; and
the muscles would stretch, bend, writhe and
turn until his heels were drawn up to the nape
of his neck, and then he would leap up in the
air and immediately fall down again. And
as St Francis was at table, he heard from the
brothers of the miserable and incurable state

of their companion, and being moved with
compassion he took a slice of bread that he
was eating, and made the sign of the most
holy Cross thereon with his holy hands that
had the sacred stigmas, and sent it to the sick
brother, who, as soon as he had eaten it, was
perfectly cured, and never more felt aught of
his infirmity.

And the next morning having come, he
sent two brothers who were of that house to
Alvernia, that they might stay there, and
with them he sent back the peasant who had
come along with his ass which they had bor-
rowed, desiring that he should return in their
company to his home. And after remaining
a few days longer in the same house, he departed and went on to the city of Castello.
And behold, many of the townsfolk came
to meet him, bringing with them a woman
that a long time had been possessed of the
devil, and humbly prayed him for her deliver-
ance; because by her doleful howling and
barking like a dog, and piercing shrieks, she
disturbed the whole country round. Then St
Francis, having first prayed and made on her
the sign of the most holy Cross, commanded
the devil to come out of her; and immediately he departed from her, leaving her sound
in mind and body. And she, having told this
miracle to all the people, behold another
woman, with great faith, brought him her
child, who was dangerously ill with a cruel
wound in his body, and fervently besought
him to make the holy sign on it with his

P

hands.   Then St Francis, in answer to her
devotion, took the child and removed the
bandages from his wound, making the sign of
the most holy cross three times upon it, and
then, with his own hands, replaced the bandages and gave him back to his mother. And
because it was evening she put him immediately to bed that he might sleep. And in the
morning, when she went to get him up, she
found the bandages gone ; and looking upon
him, she saw that he was perfectly healed as
though he had never ailed aught, except that
where the wound had been the flesh had
grown together like to a crimson rose—and
this rather in testimony to the miracle than
as a result of the wound, for this same rose
remained with him all his life long, and produced in him a special devotion to St Francis
every time he looked upon it.

In this town St Francis sojourned for a
month at the entreaty of the devout citizens,
during which time he performed many more
miracles ; and after this he departed and went
on his way to St Mary of the Angels, with
Brother Leo and with a good man who had
lent him another ass on which he rode. And
it came to pass that because of the bad roads
and the inclement weather, though they
journeyed on all day, they could not reach
the house where they were to remain the
night; therefore, constrained by the darkness
and the storm, they took shelter for the night
which was coming on, and from the snow
which was beginning to fall, in a hollow cave

in the rock. And as they lay thus, with much
inconvenience and badly covered, the good
man to whom the ass belonged could not
sleep for the cold ; and as there was no means
of making a fire, he began to complain bitterly within himself and to lament and murmur against St Francis, who had led him into
such a place. Then St Francis, perceiving
this, had compassion on him ; and in the fervour of his charity put out his hand, and
touched him on his ; when behold, a new
wonder! immediately he touched him with
that hand which was seared and pierced with
the fire of the seraph, the cold completely
vanished ; and such a warmth entered into
the man, as it seemed to him both from before
and behind, that it was as though he were
near to the mouth of a burning furnace. And
feeling himself entirely comforted in body
and in soul, he fell asleep until the morning ;
and more sweetly, according to his own account, did he sleep there that night amongst
rocks and snow than ever in his own bed.

On the following day they journeyed on
again, and reached St Mary of the Angels.
And when they had come near unto it,
Brother Leo lifted up his eyes and looked
towards the house, and saw a most beautiful
cross, and on it the form of the Crucified,
going before St Francis, and in such a manner that, as he followed after it, when he went
on it went on, and when he stayed it stayed ;
and such was the splendour and brightness
of this cross that not only did the face of St

Francis shine with it, but also all the way
before and behind them was illumined by it;
and it disappeared only as they entered the
house of St Mary of the Angels. Then St
Francis and Brother Leo were received by
the brothers with exceeding great joy and
fraternal charity; and from that time St
Francis spent the most of his days in the
house of St Mary of the Angels until the day
of his death. And the fame of his sanctity
and of his miracles spread continually more
and more throughout the order and throughout the world, although in his profound humility he concealed as well as he could the
grace and the gift of God, calling himself the
greatest of sinners.

St Francis, seeing that through the stigmas his bodily strength grew less and less, so
that he could no longer undertake the care of
the order, summoned the general chapter;
and when it was assembled, he humbly excused himself before his brethren for his in-
ability to continue to have the oversight of
the order in so far as to fulfil the office of
general; not that he entirely renounced the
office, because, having been made general
by the pope, he could not give up his office
or substitute a successor without the pope's
express permission; but he chose for his
vicar Brother Pietro Cattani, commending
the care of the order to him and to the ministers of the provinces with all the affection
that he could. And having done this he was
comforted in spirit, and raised his hand and

his eyes to heaven, and said : " To Thee, O Lord my God, to Thee I commend Thy family, which thou hast committed unto me until this hour when, by reason of my infirmity which Thou knowest, O my sweetest Lord, I can no longer sustain the care of it. I commend it also to the ministers of the provinces ; they shall answer for it at the day of judgment if any brother, by their negligence or by their bad example or their too harsh correction, should perish." And through these words it pleased God that all the brothers assembled together should understand that he spoke of the holy stigmas when he excused himself on account of his infirmity ; and for the great devotion that they felt, none of them could refrain from weeping. And from this time forth he left all the care of the government of the order in the hands of his vicar and of the ministers of the provinces, and said : " Now that I have given up the charge of the order on account of my infirmity, I have henceforth nothing more to do but to pray for it, and to give a good example to the brothers. And I know of a truth that even if my infirmity were to depart, the greatest help that I could give to the order would be to pray to God continually for it, that He would defend and govern and preserve it."

Now, as has already been said, although St Francis was ingenious in hiding as much as possible the most holy stigmas, and ever since he had received them went always

with his hands bandaged and his feet
covered, he was not able to prevent many
brothers from seeing and touching them in
divers manners, and more especially the
wound in his side, which he tried with the
greatest diligence to conceal. Thus a
brother who was serving him induced him
one day by a pious strategy to take off his
tunic that he might shake the dust out of it.
And whilst St Francis did so, as he stood
by, he saw plainly the wound in his side;
and putting his hand quickly on his breast
he touched the wound with his three fingers
and measured its depth and breadth; and
after a similar manner his vicar, Pietro
Cattani, saw it also.

But Brother Ruffino saw it and was
assured of it more plainly still. He was a
man of the most profound contemplation,
on which account St Francis said of him
more than once that there was not in the
whole world a man more holy than he; and
on account of his sanctity St Francis loved
him with an intimate affection and let him
do in all as he would. This Brother Ruffino
assured himself in three distinct ways
amongst others of the most holy stigmas,
and especially of that in the side. The
first was, that having to wash the nether
garments, which St Francis wore large
enough to be drawn over the wound in the
right side so as to cover it, he examined
and considered them attentively, and each
time found them covered with blood on the

right side, by which he knew certainly that the blood continued to flow from the wound; and for this St Francis reproved him when he saw that he pried into the garments which he laid off in order to discover this sign. The second manner that the said Brother Ruffino employed was, that with great care one day he thrust his fingers into the wound, at which St Francis for the pain he felt cried out: " God forgive thee, Brother Ruffino, that thou hast done this unto me ! " The third manner was, that with great instance he besought St Francis one day, as the greatest favour, to give him his cloak and take his instead, for the love of charity. And the father, full of charity consenting, although unwillingly, taking off his cloak gave it to him, and received his in its place; and during this taking off and changing of habits Brother Ruffino plainly saw the wound.

In like manner Brother Leo and many other brothers saw these sacred stigmas of St Francis during his lifetime; which brothers—although on account of their sanctity they were worthy of belief on their simple word, yet to prevent all possibility of doubt—took their oath on the holy Gospels as to what they had clearly seen. Several cardinals also, who were intimate with him, saw the holy stigmas, and wrote pious and eloquent hymns, antiphons and proses on them. And Pope Alexander himself, preaching on one occasion to a large audience where all the cardinals were present, and amongst others the holy Brother Bonaventure, said and affirmed that he had seen with his own eyes the sacred stigmas of St Francis during his lifetime. And the Lady Jacopa di Settesoli of Rome, who was the first lady of her time in Rome and most devoted to St Francis, saw them and kissed them several times with great reverence both before and after his death; for which cause she came from Rome to Assisi by divine revelation to be present at his death, which happened in this wise :

A few days before he died, St Francis was taken ill at Assisi in the palace of the bishop, where he was staying with several of his companions ; and notwithstanding all his sickness he sang continually the praises of Jesus Christ. Now on a certain day one of his companions said to him : " Father, thou knowest that the citizens here have great faith in thee, and hold thee to be a holy man ; wherefore they may think that, if thou art what they think thee to be, thou shouldst begin in this sickness to think of thy death, and rather weep than sing, inasmuch as thy sickness is very grave. And know that thy singing and ours, as thou wilt have us join in, is heard by many both in the palace and outside, because this palace is guarded on thy account by many armed men, who might take bad example from what thou doest ; it seems to me thou wouldst do well to depart from here, and let

us all return to St Mary of the Angels, for we
are not in our place here amongst seculars."
Then St Francis answered him: "My beloved
brother, thou knowest how two years ago,
when we were at Foligno, God revealed to
thee, and afterwards also to me, the time of
my death, according to which in a few days
my life must end in this sickness; and in the
same revelation God gave me the assurance
of the remission of all my sins, and of an entrance into the bliss of paradise.   Before this
revelation was given me, I wept at the thought
of death and of my sins, but ever since I am
so full of joy that it is impossible for me to
weep, and therefore I sing and will sing to
God, who has given me the treasure of His
grace and made me certain of the eternal
treasure of the glory of paradise.   As to our
departing from here, I consent and am well
pleased at it; only do thou find means of con-
veying me, for because of my sickness I can
no longer walk." Then the brothers took him
up in their arms, and carried him away accompanied by many of the citizens.

    And when they had come near to a hospice
which stood by the way, St Francis said to
them that carried him : " Let me down on the
ground, and turn my face towards the city."
And when it was done, so that he looked towards Assisi, he blessed it with many blessings, saying : " Blessed be thou of God, O
holy city, because by thee shall many souls
be saved, and in thee many servants of God
shall dwell, and from out of thee shall many

be elected to the kingdom of eternal life."
And having said these words, he had himself
carried on to St Mary of the Angels.
And when they had arrived, they carried
him into the infirmary, and laid him down to
rest. Then St Francis called to him one of
his companions, and said : "My beloved
brother, God has revealed to me that in this
sickness, after a few days, I shall pass away
from this life; and thou knowest that the Lady
Jacopa di Settesoli, who is so greatly devoted
to our order, if she heard of my death and was
not present at it, would have overmuch sorrow; therefore send her word that if she would
see me alive she should come at once." To
which the brother replied : "True, father ;
and indeed, for the great devotion she has for
thee, it would ill beseem that she should not
be here at thy death." "Go therefore," said
St Francis, "and bring me ink, pen and
paper, and write as I shall tell thee."
    And when he had brought them, St
Francis dictated the letter to him thus : "To
the Lady Jacopa, servant of God, Brother
Francis, the poor little one of Christ, saluta-
tion and fellowship of the Holy Spirit and of
our Lord Jesus Christ. Know, beloved, that
Christ the blessed has revealed to me by His
grace that the end of my life is at hand. And
therefore if thou wouldst still find me alive, as
soon as thou shalt receive this letter arise and
come to St Mary of the Angels ; because if
thou come not speedily thou wilt not find me
here ; and bring with thee a shroud to wrap

my body in, and the wax which will be needed
for my burial. I pray thee also to bring me
some of that food which thou wert wont to
give me when I was sick at Rome." And
when this letter was written, it was revealed
to St Francis from God that the Lady Jacopa
was on her way to him, and was already near
to the house, and that she had brought with
her all those things which he had asked in
the letter. Therefore he told the brother who
wrote it to write no further for there was no
need, and to keep back the letter; at which the
brother marvelled that he should not finish
the letter and despatch it. And while he
waited a little space, there came a loud knocking at the door, and St Francis sent the porter
to open it; and behold there stood at the door
the Lady Jacopa, the noblest lady in Rome,
with her two sons, Roman senators, and a
great company of men on horseback; and
entering, the Lady Jacopa went straight to
St Francis in the infirmary. At this meeting
St Francis had great joy and consolation, and
so had the lady also, seeing him alive and
able to speak. Then she recounted to him
that, being still in Rome, God had revealed to
her whilst she was at prayer the speedy ter-
mination of his life, and that he would ask of
her those things which she had brought with
her. And she had them carried in to St Francis, and persuaded him that he should eat.

And when he had eaten and was much refreshed, the Lady Jacopa knelt down at his
feet, and embracing those most holy feet

sealed and adorned with the wounds of Jesus
Christ, she kissed them, and bathed them
with her tears with such excess of devotion
that the brothers thought verily they beheld
the Magdalene at the feet of Christ, and by no
means whatever could they draw her away.
At last, after a great while they raised her,
and drew her aside, and asked of her how she
had arrived so opportunely, and brought with
her all those things which were needful to St
Francis, both for the remaining space of his
life and for his burial. Then the Lady Jacopa
told them how that one night in Rome, whilst
she was praying, she heard a voice from
heaven, which said : "If thou wouldst see St
Francis alive, go without delay, and take with
thee those things thou hast given him before
when he was sick, and those things also which
will be needed for his burial ; " and she said :
" I have done so." And she remained there
until St Francis had passed from this life and
was buried. And at his burial she with all her
company paid him the greatest honours, and
at her own expense. And returning to Rome,
within a little time after this noble lady died
a holy death, and out of her devotion to St
Francis directed that she should be carried
to St Mary of the Angels and buried there ;
and so it was done.

After the death of St Francis, not only did
the Lady Jacopa see and kiss his glorious
sacred stigmas, but many citizens of Assisi
also did the same ; and amongst them a
certain cavalier, a great man and of great

renown named Jeronimo, who had much
doubted and was incredulous concerning
them, even as St Thomas the Apostle doubted
of those of Christ Himself. And in order to
assure himself and others, he ventured, in the
presence of the brothers and many seculars,
to move about the nails in the hands and feet,
and to feel the depth of the wound in the side.
After which trial, he bore testimony to the
fact, swearing on the Gospels that so it was,
and that he had seen and touched them. St
Clare also and her religious, being present at
his burial, saw and kissed the glorious sacred
stigmas of St Francis.

V—Of the Fifth Consideration of the Holy Stigmas

THIS last consideration contains certain
visions and miracles which God wrought and
manifested after the death of St Francis, for
the confirmation of his having received the
most holy stigmas, and in order to fix the day
and the hour in which he received them from
Christ.

And in the first place it must be related
how in the year of our Lord 1282 in the month
of October, Brother Philip, minister of Tuscany, by command of Brother John Buona-
grazia, the minister general, required under
holy obedience of Brother Matthew of Cas-
tiglione, a man of great devotion and sanctity,
that he should tell what he knew of the day
and the hour when the most holy stigmas of

Christ were impressed on the body of St Francis, as it was known that he had had revelations concerning it. The same Brother Matthew, constrained by holy obedience, replied in this manner : " When I was in the community of Alvernia last year in the month of May, I was praying in the cell where it is believed the seraphic apparition took place. And in my prayer, I earnestly begged of God that it would please Him to reveal to some one the day and the hour and the place in which the most holy stigmas were impressed on the body of St Francis. And as I persevered in this prayer until after the first watch of the night, St Francis appeared to me in a very great light, and said to me : ' Son, for what dost thou ask God ? ' And I answered him : ' Father, I have asked for such and such things.' And he said to me : ' I am Francis, thy father, dost thou know me well ?' ' Father,' said I to him, ' I do.'

" Then he showed me the sacred stigmas in his hands and feet and side, and said : ' The time has come when God wills, for His great glory, to manifest what hitherto the brothers have not bestirred themselves to inquire into. Know then that he who appeared to me was not an angel but Jesus Christ Himself under the form of a seraph, who impressed with His own hands on my body these very wounds, such as He had received them in His own Body on the cross. And it was in this wise : The day before that on which is kept the Exaltation of the Holy Cross, an angel came

to me and told me on the part of God that
I should prepare myself with patience to receive that which God would send me. And I
answered that I was ready to receive and to
endure whatever it should please God to send.
Then the next morning, which was the morning of the feast of the Holy Cross and which
that year fell on a Friday, I came out of my
cell at dawn in great fervour of spirit, and betook myself to prayer in the place where thou
now art, in which place I often prayed. And
as I prayed, behold there descended through
the air from heaven, with great impetus, a
young man crucified, in the form of a seraph
with six wings. At this marvellous sight I
knelt down humbly, and began to contemplate with devotion the immeasurable love of
Jesus Christ crucified and the immeasurable
pain of His Passion : and the sight of Him
produced in me such a great compassion that
it seemed to me as though I felt His very
Passion in my own body; and at His presence
all this mountain became resplendent as the
sun; and He descended and came close to me.
And standing before me, He spoke to me
certain secret words, which as yet I have revealed to none; but the time is near when
they shall be revealed. Then after a little
space Christ departed from me and returned
into heaven, and I found myself marked with
these wounds. Go therefore,' said St Francis,
' and assure thy minister of these things, because this is the work of God and not of man.'
And having said these words, St Francis

blessed me, and returned to heaven with a great multitude of youths in shining raiment." All these things the said Brother Matthew declared he had heard and seen, not sleeping but waking. And afterwards he took a solemn oath that he had told these things, under holy obedience, to the said minister in his cell at Florence.

How a holy Brother prayed God that he might know the secret Words spoken by the Seraph, and how St Francis himself revealed them to him

ON another occasion a devout and holy brother, whilst reading the legend of St Francis, in the chapter where is related the history of the sacred stigmas, began to think, with great anxiety of spirit, what might be the words concerning those secret things which the seraph spoke to St Francis when he appeared to him, and which St Francis had said he would never reveal to anyone as long as he lived. And thus the brother said within himself: "These words St Francis would not repeat to any one during his lifetime, but after the death of his body perhaps he might relate them if he were devoutly asked to do so." And from that time the devout brother began to pray to God and St Francis that it would please them to reveal these words; and having persevered eight years in this prayer, in the eighth year he merited to have it answered; and in this wise:

One day after they had dined and returned thanks in the church, he remained praying in another part of the church by himself; and as he prayed to God and St Francis for this cause, with more than his usual fervour and with many tears, another brother called him, and commanded him on the part of the guardian to accompany him to the fields for the affairs of the house. At which, not doubting but that obedience is more meritorious than prayer, immediately he had heard the command of the superior he humbly left off praying and went with the brother who had called him; and as it pleased God by this act of prompt obedience he merited that which by his protracted praying he had not obtained. For now as they both went out of the door of the house they met two strange friars, who appeared to have come from a far country; one of them seemed to be young and the other old and emaciated, and both of them, through the bad weather, were wet through and covered with mud. Wherefore this obedient brother had great compassion for them, and said to the brother whom he was accompanying: " O beloved brother, would that the business on which we are going could be delayed a little, for these strange brothers have great need to be charitably received. I pray thee let me go first and wash their feet, and especially the feet of the aged brother who has the greatest need, and do thou wash those of the younger, and after-

Q

wards we can go on the business of the convent." Then the other brother consenting to the charity of his companion, they returned to the convent, and received these strange brothers with great charity, and led them to the fire in the kitchen that they might warm and dry themselves, where also eight brothers belonging to the house were warming themselves.

And when they had sat awhile by the fire, they led them apart to wash their feet as they had agreed to do. And as the obedient brother was washing the feet of the elder of the two and removing the mud with which they were covered, he looked and saw that they were marked with the most holy stigmas; and immediately with joy and wonder he devoutly embraced them and cried out: "Either thou art Christ, or thou art St Francis!" At the sound of his voice and of these words all the brothers who were by the fire arose and came with haste, and beheld with great fear and trembling those glorious stigmas. Then the aged brother, at their entreaty, suffered the friars to see them clearly, to touch and to kiss them. And as they wondered yet more and more, and were filled with joy, he said to them : " Doubt not, and do not fear, most beloved brothers and my sons; I am your father, Brother Francis who by the will of God founded three orders. And because I have been entreated these eight years by this brother, who has just washed

my feet, and to-day more fervently than at
other times that I would reveal to him the
secret words which the seraph spoke to me
when he gave me the stigmas, which words
I never would reveal in my lifetime, to-day,
by the commandment of God, for the sake of
his perseverance and of his prompt obedience by which he has given up the sweetness of contemplation, I am sent by God to
reveal to you what he has asked."

And turning to the said friars St Francis
said thus : " Know, most beloved brothers,
that being on the mountain of Alvernia,
wholly absorbed in the contemplation of
the Passion of Christ, in that seraphic
vision I was thus stigmatized in my own
body by Christ Himself; and He said to
me : 'Knowest thou what I have done to
thee ? I have given thee the marks of My
Passion that thou mayest be My standard-
bearer. And as I, on the day of My death,
descended into Limbo, and, by virtue of My
stigmas, liberated all the souls I found
there and conducted them to paradise, so
also I grant to thee in this hour, in order
that thou mayest be conformed to Me in thy
death even as thou hast been in thy life,
that when thou shalt have passed away
from this life, every year on the anniversary
of thy death thou shalt go into purgatory,
and, by virtue of these stigmas which I
have given thee, shalt liberate all the souls
thou shalt find there belonging to thy three
orders, Friars Minor, sisters and virgins,

and over and above these all who have
been devout to thee, and shalt lead them to
paradise.' These words of Christ I never
revealed whilst I lived in this world." And
having thus spoken St Francis and his
companion suddenly disappeared. And
many brothers afterwards heard these
things from the eight brothers who were
present during the vision and had heard the
words of St Francis.

How St Francis after his Death appeared to Brother John of Alvernia

ST FRANCIS appeared on another occasion,
on Mount Alvernia, to Brother John of
Alvernia, a man of great sanctity, whilst he
was in prayer, and spoke with him for a
long time. And at last as he was about to
depart, he said to him : "Ask of me what
thou wilt." And Brother John said :
"Father, I pray thee that thou wouldst tell
me what I have desired to know for a long
time, where thou wert and what thou wert
doing when the seraph appeared to thee."
Then St Francis answered : "I was praying in that place where stands the chapel of
Count Simon of Battifolle, and asked two
graces of my Lord Jesus Christ; the first
was that He would grant me in this life to
feel in my soul and in my body, so far as
possible, all the pains that He Himself felt
during the time of His bitter Passion. The
second grace which I asked of Him was like

unto the first, that I might feel in my heart
the excessive love which induced Him to
suffer such a Passion for us sinners. And
then God put it into my heart that He
would give me to feel both the one and the
other in so far as it was possible for a mere
creature; which thing indeed was fulfilled
in me by the impression of the stigmas."

Brother John asked him again if the
secret words which the seraph had spoken
to him were such as had been related by the
holy brother aforesaid, who affirmed that he
had so heard them from St Francis in the
presence of eight brothers. And St Francis
replied that this was the truth as the brother had said. Then Brother John, taking
courage through this general condescension
to his requests, said: "O father, I beseech
thee let me see and kiss thy most holy and
glorious stigmas, not that I doubt of aught,
but solely for my consolation and because
I have always so greatly desired this
favour." And St Francis with good will
showed them and presented them to him,
so that he both clearly saw and touched,
and also kissed them.

And finally Brother John asked: "Father,
what consolation didst thou not feel in thy
soul when thou didst see Christ the blessed
coming to thee to give thee the marks of His
most sacred Passion? Would to God that I
might feel a little of the sweetness thereof!"
And St Francis answered: "Seest thou these
nails?" Brother John said: "Yes, father."

"Touch once again," said St Francis, "this nail in my hand." Then Brother John with great reverence and fear touched the nail, and as soon as he had touched it there came forth so great a fragrance like to a cloud of incense, that, entering by his nostrils, it filled his soul and his body with such sweetness that immediately he was ravished in ecstasy and became insensible; and thus he remained rapt in God from the hour of terce, when this took place, until vespers. And Brother John never spoke of this vision and familiar conversation with St Francis except to his confessor until he came to die; when, being near to death, he revealed it to several of the brothers. 🌿

How a holy Brother saw a wonderful Vision concerning one of his Companions who was dead

IN the province of Rome there was a certain holy and devout brother who saw the following wonderful vision. One of his best-beloved companions amongst the brothers, having died in the night, was buried on the following morning at the entrance to the choir. And on the same day this brother withdrew himself into a corner of the choir with the devout intention of praying to God and St Francis for the soul of the departed brother, his companion. And as he persevered with prayers and tears in his supplications till mid-day, when all the others had gone to sleep, he suddenly heard a great

noise in the cloister. At which he turned
his eyes in affright towards the sepulchre of
his brother; and he saw, standing in the entrance to the choir, St Francis, and behind
him a great multitude of brothers around the
sepulchre. Looking further he saw in the
midst of the cloisters a great fire, and in the
midst of the flames thereof the soul of his
departed companion. And looking back
again he saw Jesus Christ walking within
the cloisters with a great multitude of angels
and saints.

He beheld these things in great amazement, and he saw that when Christ passed
in front of the choir St Francis with all his
brothers knelt down, and said thus : " I pray
Thee, my dearest Lord and Father, by that
inestimable charity Thou didst show to the
human race in Thine incarnation that Thou
wouldst have mercy on the soul of my brother
that burns in yonder flame; " and Christ
answered nothing, but passed on. And as
He returned a second time and passed in
front of the choir, St Francis knelt again
with his brothers, as at the first time, and
prayed again in this manner : " I pray Thee,
most compassionate Father and Lord, by the
immeasurable charity which Thou didst show
to the generations of men when Thou didst
die on the wood of the cross, that Thou
wouldst have mercy on the soul of my
brother." And again Christ passed as before,
as though He heard him not. And as He
went round the cloisters He returned a third

time, and passed in front of the choir, and then St Francis kneeling, as at the first, showed Him his hands and his feet and his breast, and said: "I pray Thee, most compassionate Father and Lord, by the great pains and great consolation which I sustained when Thou didst impress these stigmas on my flesh, that Thou wouldst have mercy on the soul of my brother that is in this fire of purgatory." O wonder! As St Francis thus besought Christ the third time, and prayed for the sake of his stigmas to be heard, immediately He stood still, and looking on the stigmas He said: "Francis, to thee I concede the soul of thy brother." And by this He certainly wished to honour and confirm the glorious stigmas of St Francis, and evidently to testify that the souls of his brothers who enter purgatory can by no means more quickly be delivered from their pains, and conducted into the glories of paradise, than by virtue of those stigmas, according to the words which Christ spoke to St Francis when He imprinted them upon him. For as soon as He had spoken these words, the fire disappeared from the cloisters, and the soul of him that was dead came to St Francis, and together with him and with Christ, and with all that blessed company following their glorious King, went up into heaven. At which his brother who had prayed for him, seeing him freed from his pains and conducted to paradise, was filled with the greatest joy, and went and told the other brothers

all the vision as it befel him ; and they, with
him, praised and returned thanks to God.

**How a noble Knight devoted to St Francis was
assured of his Death and of the sacred Stigmas**

A NOBLE knight of Massa di San Pietro,
named Landolfo, who was specially devoted
to St Francis and had received from him the
habit of the third order, was assured of the
death of the saint and of the truth of the most
sacred and glorious stigmas in the following manner. When St Francis was near to
death, the devil entered into a certain woman
who lived in the castle of Landolfo and
cruelly tormented her, causing her to speak
with so much subtlety that she vanquished all
the scholars and men of letters who came to
dispute with her. And it came to pass that
the devil left her free for two days, and returned on the third to afflict her more cruelly
than at first. Then Landolfo, hearing of this,
went to the woman, and questioned the foul
spirit that dwelt in her as to the reason why
he had thus departed for two days, and returned on the third to torment her more
vigorously than before. And the demon
answered : " When I left her, it was because
I, with all my companions who are in these
parts, assembled together, and went in great
force to the death of the beggar, Francis, to
dispute with him and to take his soul ; but he
being surrounded and defended by a greater
multitude of angels and carried by them

straight into heaven, we returned in confusion; wherefore I returned and rendered to this miserable woman that which I had left undone for two days."

Then Landolfo abjured him, in the name of God, to tell the truth as to the sanctity of St Francis, whom he affirmed to be dead, and of St Clare, who was living. And the demon replied: "Whether I will or no, I must speak that which is the truth. God the eternal Father was so incensed against the sins of the world that it appears He would, within a little time, have pronounced the final sentence against the men and women in it, and have exterminated them unless they repented. But Christ His Son, praying for the sinners, promised to renew His own life and His Passion in a man, namely in Francis, the poor little beggar, by whose life and doctrine many should be brought back to the way of truth, and many also to do penance. And lo! in order to show the world that which He had done in St Francis, He willed that the stigmas and signs of His Passion, which He had impressed upon his body during his life, should be seen and touched by many after his death. Likewise also, the Mother of Christ promised to renew her virginal purity and humility in a woman, namely in Sister Clare, insomuch that she should reclaim many thousands of women from our hands. And thus God the Father, being appeased by these promises, suspended His final sentence."

Then Landolfo, wishing to know for certain whether the devil, who is the source and the father of lies, had spoken the truth in this matter, and especially as to the death of St Francis, sent one of his trusted attendants to Assisi, to St Mary of the Angels, to know whether St Francis were living or dead. When the said attendant arrived, he found it so of a truth, and returning to his lord told him that precisely at the day and hour that the devil had said St Francis had passed away from this life.

How Pope Gregory IX, having doubted of the Stigmas, was enlightened concerning them

LEAVING aside all the miracles which are recorded of the most holy stigmas of St Francis and which are to be read in his legend, it remains to relate in conclusion of this fifth consideration how Pope Gregory IX, doubting somewhat of the wound in the side of St Francis, as he himself afterwards related, saw St Francis in a vision one night, lifting his right arm a little and showing him the wound in his side. After which he asked for a phial, which being brought St Francis placed it under the wound; and it seemed to the pope in very deed that it was filled to the brim with blood mingled with water flowing from the wound; and from that hour all doubt departed from him. And afterwards, with the

counsel of all the cardinals, he approved
the sacred and holy stigmas of St Francis,
and in consideration of them granted to the
brothers special privileges by a papal bull,
and this he did at Viterbo in the eleventh
year of his pontificate; and also in the
twelfth year he granted still greater privileges. Furthermore Pope Nicholas III and
Pope Alexander granted copious privileges,
according to which any one denying the
most holy stigmas of St Francis might be
proceeded against as a heretic.

And here ends the fifth consideration on
the sacred and glorious stigmas of our
father St Francis, whose life may God give
us grace to follow in this world, that by the
virtue of the same glorious stigmas we may
merit to be saved and to be with him in
paradise. To the praise of Jesus Christ, and
of His poor little one, St Francis. Amen.

The Life of Brother Juniper

How Brother Juniper cut off the Foot of a Pig to give to one who was sick

ONE of the most chosen disciples and first companions of St Francis was a certain Brother Juniper, a man of profound humility, of great fervour and charity, with regard to whom St Francis said once, speaking with some of his saintly companions : " He would be a good Friar Minor who had conquered the world and himself like Brother Juniper."

It came to pass once at St Mary of the Angels that, inflamed with the love of God, he went to visit a sick brother, and with great compassion asked him : "Can I do you any service?" The patient replied : "It would be a great comfort to me if you could get me a pig's foot to eat." Immediately Brother Juniper said : "Leave it to me, you shall have it at once." Away he goes and snatches a knife from the kitchen, and runs in fervour of spirit to the wood where a number of pigs were feeding, and having thrown himself upon one of them cuts off its foot and flees, leaving the pig thus mutilated. He returns and washes and dresses and cooks the foot and, with much diligence having well prepared it, he bears it with great charity to the invalid, who ate it with avidity to the great consolation and joy of Brother Juniper, whilst he in high spirits, to amuse the sick man, recounted his assault on the pig.

In the meantime the keeper of the pigs, who had seen him cutting off the foot, went and told the whole affair in detail with great indignation to his master, who, when he had heard it, came to the house of the brothers, calling them hypocrites, thieves, liars, rascals and good-for-nothings, and saying : " Why did you cut off my pig's foot ? " At the great disturbance which he made, St Francis came out with all the brothers, and humbly excusing himself and them, as ignorant of what had happened, tried to pacify him by promising to compensate him to the last farthing. But for all this the man was not pacified, but went away in a rage, still uttering menaces and threats and repeating over and over how maliciously they had cut off the foot of his pig. And listening neither to excuse nor promise, he departed as angry as he came, leaving all the brothers stupefied and amazed.

But St Francis, full of prudence, thought it over and said in his heart : " Can Brother Juniper have done this through indiscreet zeal ? " And he had Brother Juniper called to him secretly, and asked him, saying : " Did you cut off the foot of a pig in the wood ? " And Brother Juniper, not as one who had committed a fault but rather as one who had performed a great act of charity, answered him joyously : " It is true, sweet father mine, that I cut off the foot of a pig,

and for the reason be pleased to listen, my
father, feelingly. I went out of charity to
visit the sick brother;" and then he told
him in detail all he had done, and added:
"I tell thee thus, that considering the consolation it brought our sick brother and the
pleasure he took in it, if I had cut off the
feet of a hundred pigs, as I did of that one,
I am sure it would have been pleasing to
God." To which St Francis, in just anger
and very great displeasure, replied: "O
Brother Juniper, why hast thou caused such
a great scandal? Not without reason does
this man complain and rail so greatly
against us; and perhaps at this moment
he is in the town spreading an accusation
against us of such ill-doing and with very
great cause. Wherefore I command thee
by holy obedience to run after him, and
overtake him, and throw thyself at his feet,
and tell him thy fault, promising to make
such satisfaction to him as that he shall
have nothing to complain of against us, for
certainly this has been too great an excess."

Brother Juniper was astonished at these
words; and full of wonder that anyone
should be angered by such an act of charity,
because it seemed to him that temporal
goods were nothing at all, except in so far
as they were charitably shared with one's
neighbour, he answered: "Doubt not, my
father, that I will soon compensate the man,
and make him content. And why should I
be troubled, seeing that this pig whose foot

I cut off belonged more to God than it did to him, and that I did it for so great a charity?" And with this he ran off, and overtook the man, who had by no means recovered his equanimity but was still angry beyond measure; and he narrated to him how and why he cut off the foot of the pig; and this with as much fervour and exultation and joy as if he had done him a great service, for which he ought to be greatly rewarded.

The man, full of anger and beside himself with fury, gave Brother Juniper many bad names, calling him a fool and a madman, a robber and the worst of brigands. But Brother Juniper cared nothing for these insulting words, and marvelled within himself, for he rejoiced in being abused; and thought he could not have well understood the man, because there seemed to him room rather for praise than for blame. So he told the story over again, and throwing himself on the man's neck, kissed and embraced him, and told him how he had done it solely out of charity, inviting and pressing him to do the same with the rest of the pigs; and with so much affection, simplicity and humility, that the man came back to himself, and not without many tears fell on his knees and acknowledged his own fault in speaking and acting so violently against the brothers; and he went and caught the pig and killed it, and having cut it up and cooked it, he bore it with much devotion and with

many tears to St Mary of the Angels, and
gave it to the holy brothers to eat in com-
pensation for the abuse he had given them.
· Then St Francis, considering the simplicity and patience under adversity of the
said holy Brother Juniper, said to his companions and the others who were present:
" Would to God, my brothers, that I had
a whole forest of such Junipers!"

An Instance of the great Power which Brother Juniper had over the Demons

INASMUCH as the demons could not endure
the purity of Brother Juniper's innocence and
the depth of his humility, the following instance took place, by which this was most
clearly shown. A certain person who was
possessed suddenly threw himself out of the
way he was going, and, contrary to all his
usual customs, fled hither and thither by de-
vious paths for about seven miles. And when
his relatives, who pursued him, with great
grief had overtaken and interrogated him
asking why he had fled with such precipi-
tancy, he replied : " The reason is this; because that idiot Juniper was passing along the
way, and I cannot endure his presence or his
aspect, therefore I fled into the woods." And
they certified themselves of the truth that it
was even so; that Brother Juniper had passed
by at the same hour as the demon had said.
Wherefore St Francis, when they brought
him the possessed that he might heal them,

R

if the evil spirit did not immediately depart at his command used to say : "If thou depart not forthwith from this creature of God, I will fetch hither against thee Brother Juniper;" and immediately the demons, fearing the presence of Brother Juniper and unable to sustain the virtue and humility of St Francis, departed from them.

How Brother Juniper, at the instigation of the Devil, was condemned to the gibbet

ONCE on a time, the devil wishing to terrify Brother Juniper and to give him vexation and tribulation, went to a most cruel tyrant, called Nicholas, who was then at war with the city of Viterbo, and said : " My lord, guard well your castle, because presently there will come hither from Viterbo a notorious traitor to put you to death, and set fire to your castle. And you shall know the truth of this by these signs : He is attired as a harmless beggar, his clothes all ragged and tattered and his hood falling in shreds upon his shoulders ; and he carries with him an awl with which he is to take your life, and a tinder box with which he is to set fire to the castle; if you do not find all this true make an example of me." Hearing this, Nicholas had great fear, because he that told him these things seemed to be a man of weight and character. And he commanded that the guard should be set with diligence, and that, if any man answer-

ing to this description appeared, he should
immediately be brought before him.

Soon after, Brother Juniper came by alone,
for, on account of his great perfection, he had
leave to go out and to come in as he pleased.
He was met first by some evil youths, who
began to deride and to make a fool of him.
He was not at all disturbed at this, but
rather invited them to mock him the more.
And when he arrived at the castle gates, the
guards, seeing him so ill-favoured with his
clothing all torn and ragged, for he had given
part of his habit away on the road to the poor
for the love of God and had no appearance of
a Friar Minor about him, and because the
signs they were given to expect seemed manifest upon him, with great fury seized him, and
led him before their master, the tyrant Nicholas. And having searched him for arms they
found in his sleeve an awl, with which he used
to mend his sandals; and a flint, which he
carried in order to make a fire, when he remained, as he oftentimes did, in the woods
and deserts.

Then Nicholas, seeing the signs which he
was to expect according to the testimony of
the accusing devil, commanded that they
should bind him with cords; and this was
done with so much cruelty that they entered
even into his flesh. Then he had him put upon
the rack, and his arms dragged back and dis-
located, and all his body tortured without
mercy. And being asked who he was, he replied: "I am a very great sinner." Then they

asked him, further, if he had come to betray the castle, and give it up to the Viterbese; and he answered : " I am a great traitor, and unworthy of any mercy." And they asked him if he had meant with that awl to take the life of their master, Nicholas, and to set fire to his castle; and he replied : " Much worse things would I do if God permitted it." Then Nicholas, overcome with anger, stopped the examination, and without further ceremony in hot haste condemned Brother Juniper, as a traitor and homicide, to be tied to the tail of a horse and dragged along the ground to the gallows, and then to be hanged by the neck. And Brother Juniper made no defence, but as one who, for the love of God, contents himself in adversity, remained altogether joyful and at peace. But as they carried into execution the commands of their master and tied him by the feet to the tail of a horse and dragged him along the ground, he neither complained, nor bewailed himself, but like a gentle lamb led to the slaughter, so he went with all humility. And all the people ran together to this spectacle, to see such hasty justice and cruel vengeance executed on him ; but no one recognized him.

Nevertheless, as God willed it, a good man, who had seen Brother Juniper captured and so hastily condemned, ran to the house of the Friars Minor, and said : " For the love of God I beseech you come quickly, for an unfortunate man has just been seized, and on the instant sentenced and led away to death ; come

without delay that he may place his soul in
safety in your hands, for he appears to me to
be a good man, and no time has been given
him to make his confession, but he is led already to the gallows and seems neither to
care for death nor for the salvation of his
soul; I entreat you to come quickly." The
guardian, who was a compassionate man, departed in haste to secure the man's salvation;
but when he got there, the crowd of people
who had come to see the execution was so
great that he could not push his way through.
And as he waited and watched for the
moment when he might do so, he heard a
voice from amongst the people cry : " Stay,
stay, wretches ! you hurt my legs." At the
sound of his voice the guardian thought he
recognized Brother Juniper; and, throwing
himself with all his might into the crowd, he
got through, and, removing the covering
from his face, saw that it was in truth Brother
Juniper; and in his compassion he would
have taken off his own habit and clothed him
with it ; but Brother Juniper, with a cheerful
countenance and beginning to laugh, said :
" O guardian, you are too fat, it would look
ill to see you naked; I will not have it."

Then the guardian, with many tears, entreated the executioners and all the people to
delay a little whilst he went and prayed the
tyrant Nicholas to pardon him. And the
executioners, thinking it was a relation of his
and consenting to wait a few moments, the
devoted and afflicted guardian, weeping bit-

terly, went to Nicholas, and said : " My lord, I am in such grief and amazement that my tongue refuses to speak, for here in this territory is committed to-day the greatest sin and the greatest wrong that has ever been done from the days of our fathers ; and I believe it must have been done through ignorance." Nicholas heard him patiently, and said : " What is this great wrong and evil which is committed to-day in this territory ? " The guardian answered : " My lord, that you have condemned to a most cruel death, and I believe without any cause, one of the holiest brothers in all the order of St Francis, to which you are singularly devoted." Then said Nicholas : " Tell me then, guardian, who is it ? for perhaps without knowing it I have done a great wrong." The guardian said to him : " He whom you have condemned to death is Brother Juniper, the companion of St Francis."

Nicholas was stupefied at these tidings, for he had heard of the fame of Brother Juniper and of his holy life ; and pale with terror he ran with the guardian to where Brother Juniper was, and unbound him from the tail of the horse, and set him free ; and before all the people he threw himself at his feet, and with many tears confessed his fault in the injury and wickedness he had perpetrated against this holy brother ; and he added : "I believe, verily, that the end of my evil life draws near, since I have outraged this holy man without any cause ; God will

let my sinful life end in a few days hence by
a dreadful death, although I did it in ignorance." And Brother Juniper pardoned him
freely ; nevertheless, God permitted that a
few days after, this tyrant Nicholas ended his
life by a cruel death. And Brother Juniper
departed, leaving all the people edified by
what they had seen.

How Brother Juniper gave to the Poor, for the love of God, all that he had in his power to give

SUCH pity and compassion had Brother
Juniper for the poor that, whenever he saw
any one naked or badly clothed, he immediately took off his tunic and the hood from
his head and gave it to them ; wherefore
the guardian forbade him under obedience
to give away the whole of his tunic or any
part of his habit to any one. It came to
pass that a few days after he met a poor
man half-naked, who prayed Brother
Juniper for an alms for the love of God ; to
whom the brother with much compassion
replied : " I have nothing I could give thee
except my tunic, and I am bound under
obedience by my superior not to give that
to any one, or even a part of my habit ; but
if you pull it off my back, I shall not resist
you."

He spoke not to the deaf ; and forthwith
the beggar pulled his tunic over his head
and went his way, leaving Brother Juniper

naked. And when he returned home they
asked him where his tunic was, to which he
replied : "A good man pulled it off my
back and went away with it." And this
virtue of compassion still growing in him,
he was no longer content with giving away
his tunic, but gave also the mantles of the
others, and the books and ornaments of the
church, and all that he could lay his hands
on to the poor. And for this reason the
brothers left nothing open or lying about,
because Brother Juniper gave everything
away for the love of God and to His praise.

How Brother Juniper detached some Bells from
the Altar, and gave them away for the love
of God

BROTHER JUNIPER was one day at Assisi
deeply meditating before the altar of the
convent; and it was near the time of the
Nativity of our Lord. Now this altar was
very richly decked and adorned; and the
sacristan begged him to remain and watch
by it, whilst he went away to get something
to eat. And as he continued in devout
meditation, a poor woman came and begged
an alms for the love of God. Then said
Brother Juniper : "Wait a little, and I will
see whether I can get thee something from
the ornaments of the altar." And there was
on this altar a fringe of gold, richly worked,
and with little silver bells of great value.
And Brother Juniper said : "These bells

are a superfluity;" and he took a knife and
cut off the whole of them, and gave them to
the poor woman out of compassion.

The sacristan had not eaten three or
four mouthfuls before he began to bethink
himself of Brother Juniper's ways, and to
misdoubt greatly what might become of the
ornaments of the altar which he had left in
his charge; he feared lest he should do
some mischief out of the excess of his
charity. And all in haste and in great
suspicion he rose from the table and went
back to the church, and looked to see if the
ornaments of his altar were safe and none
missing; and there he saw the fringe cut
up and all the bells gone; at which he was
greatly angered and scandalized. But
Brother Juniper, seeing his perturbation,
said : " Do not put yourself out about these
bells, for I have given them to a poor
woman who was in the greatest need of
them ; and here they were of no use whatever, but a piece of vain and worldly pomp."
Hearing this the sacristan in much distress
immediately ran through the church and all
over the city, seeking everywhere if perchance he might find them again ; but he
neither found them nor any person who had
seen anything of them. Wherefore, returning to the convent in a rage, he took up
the fringe and carried it to the general, who
was then at Assisi, and said : " Father
general, I crave justice against Brother
Juniper who has spoilt my fringe, the best

there was in the sacristy; now see how he has cut it to pieces, and torn off all the silver bells, and says that he has given them away to a poor woman." The general answered: "Brother Juniper has not done this, but your own stupidity; for you ought to know, at this time of day, his way of going on; and I tell you that I marvel he has not given away the whole thing; but all the same, I will correct him severely for this affair." And calling all the brothers together in chapter, he summoned Brother Juniper, and in the presence of all the community rebuked him severely on account of the said silver bells; and so wroth was he that he raised his voice until it became quite hoarse.

Brother Juniper cared little or almost nothing for his words, because he delighted in reproaches and in being well abused; but he began to think of a remedy for the hoarseness of the father general; and having received his reproof, he went off to the city, and ordered a porridge to be made of flour and butter. And when a good part of the night was past he returned, lighted a candle and went with his porridge to the cell of the general, and knocked. The general opened the door, and seeing him there, with the lighted candle and the porridge in his hand, asked softly: "What is this?" Brother Juniper replied: "My father, when you reproved me to-day for my faults, I noticed that your voice became

hoarse—I think that it must have been
through excess of fatigue; and therefore I
considered how to find a remedy, and had
this porridge made for you; therefore I
pray you eat it, for I assure you it will
soften your chest and your throat." The
general answered him: "What an hour is
this to come and disturb people!" And
Brother Juniper said: "See, it is made on
purpose for you; I pray you eat it without
more ado, for it will do you a great deal of
good." But the general, angry at the late-
ness of the hour and his importunity, commanded him to be off, saying that at such
an hour he had no desire to eat, and calling
him names as a rascal and a good-for-
nothing. Brother Juniper therefore, seeing
that neither prayers nor coaxing would
move him, said: "My father, since you will
not eat, and this porridge was made on purpose for you, do this much for me: hold the
candle, and I will eat it." Then the general,
being a pious and devout man and perceiving the simplicity and piety of Brother
Juniper, and that all this was done by him
out of pure devotion, said to him: "Well,
see now, since thou wilt have it so, thou
and I will eat it together." And together
they ate the porridge with a fervent charity
each for the other; and much more were
they refreshed by each other's devotion
than they were by the bodily nourishment.

How Brother Juniper kept silence for six Months

BROTHER JUNIPER resolved once to keep silence for six months in this wise. The first day for the love of the heavenly Father; the second day for the love of Jesus Christ, His Son; the third for the love of the Holy Spirit; the fourth day out of reverence to the most holy Virgin Mary; and thus, in order, each day for love of some saint, he observed the six months' silence.

How to Resist the Temptations of the Flesh

As Brother Giles, Brother Simon of Assisi, Brother Ruffino and Brother Juniper were together one day talking of God and the salvation of their souls, Brother Giles said to the others: "What do you do in temptations of the flesh?" Brother Simon replied: "I consider the vileness and iniquity of the sin, and from this conceive such a horror of it that it makes me fly from it." Brother Ruffino said: "I throw myself down on the ground and pray so fervently, invoking the clemency of God and of the Mother of Jesus Christ, that of a sudden I feel myself liberated." Brother Juniper answered: "When I feel the tumult of the diabolical suggestions of the flesh coming on, I run at once and close the door of my heart; and to secure the fortress of my heart, I occupy myself in holy meditations and holy desires, so that

when the carnal suggestion comes and
knocks at the door I answer as it were from
within, ' Begone, for the house is full already
and can hold no more guests;' and thus I
let no evil thought enter; and this thwarts
the enemy so that he departs, not only from
me, but from all the country round." Then
Brother Giles answered and said : "Brother
Juniper, I hold with thee, for the flesh is an
enemy which cannot be resisted except by
flight; for the carnal appetite which is a
traitor within and the senses of the body
assaulting us from without are enemies too
many and too powerful to be vanquished in
any other way. And hence he who would
fight in another fashion will not often gain
the victory after the fatigues of the battle.
Let us therefore fly from this vice, and we
shall be victorious."

How Brother Juniper abased himself and gave glory to God

ONCE on a time Brother Juniper, desiring to
abase himself as much as possible, took off
all but his breeches ; and, making a parcel
of his habit and his other clothes, put it on
his head, and thus went into Viterbo to the
public square, exposed to the derision of all
who beheld him. Seeing him thus, the
children and youths, supposing him to be
out of his mind, did him much despite, throwing quantities of dirt at his back, pelting
him with stones, and pushing him hither and

thither ; and thus persecuted and derided, he
remained there the greater part of the day ;
and then returned to the convent. And when
the brothers saw him in this plight, they
were much incensed against him, chiefly
because he had gone all through the city
with his bundle of clothes upon his head.
And they reproved him sharply, making him
many reproaches. And one said: "Lock
him up;" another said: "Hang him;" and
another said : "Nothing can be too bad for
him after giving such bad example and ex-
posing himself and the whole order." And
Brother Juniper, full of joy, answered:
"Well and truly do you speak; for I am
worthy of all these punishments and even
greater."

How Brother Juniper in order to abase himself played at See-saw

As Brother Juniper was going once to Rome,
where the fame of his sanctity had already
spread abroad, many of the Romans through
their great devotion for him went forth to
meet him ; and Brother Juniper, seeing so
many people coming, planned in his mind
how to turn their reverence into emptiness
and absurdity. There were two children by
the wayside who were playing at see-saw,
having placed one piece of wood across another, and each of them holding on by one
end they went up and down. Brother Juniper therefore took one of the children off the

plank, and mounted himself, and so began
to see-saw up and down with the other.   In
the meantime the people came up and marvelled to see Brother Juniper thus engaged.
Nevertheless with great devotion they saluted
him, and waited until he should have finished
his game of see-saw, to accompany him with
all honour to the convent.   And Brother
. Juniper concerned himself but little with all
their salutations, reverence and waiting on
him, but remained much absorbed in his
balancing.   And waiting thus a great while,
some began to be annoyed and to say:
"How stupid this is !"   Others, knowing
his ways, only conceived a greater devotion
for him; but all the same they all departed,
and left Brother Juniper to his see-saw.
And when they were all gone, Brother Juniper got down, quite consoled because he had
seen that many held him for a fool.   And he
went on his way and entered Rome in all
meekness and humility, and so arrived at the
convent of the Friars Minor.

How Brother Juniper once cooked a fortnight's Dinner for the Brothers

As Brother Juniper was once staying in a
very small house belonging to the friars,
it happened that for some reason all the
brothers were obliged to go out, and only
Brother Juniper remained in the house.
Therefore the guardian said : "Brother Juniper, all of us are going out; so see that, when

we come home, you have cooked some small refreshment for the brothers on their return." And Brother Juniper replied very willingly: "Leave it all to me." When all the others were gone, said Brother Juniper to himself: "What useless care and solicitude is this, that one brother should be lost in the kitchen, and kept away from prayer! For a certainty, I am appointed to cook for this once; I will do so much at a time, that all the brothers, and more, if more there were, shall have enough for a whole fortnight." So, full of business, he went off to the farm, and brought several large earthenware pots for cooking, and procured fresh and dried meat, fowls, eggs and herbs, also firewood in plenty, and lighting his fire, put all on to boil—fowls in their feathers, and eggs in their shells, and all the other things in the same fashion.

When the brothers returned home, one of them, who was well aware of Brother Juniper's simplicity, went straight to the kitchen, and there found many and huge pots on a raging fire; and sat himself down, looking on with astonishment, and saying nothing, but watching with what solicitude Brother Juniper attended to his cooking. Because the fire was very fierce, and he could not well get near his pots to skim them, he took a plank and tied it tightly in front of him with cords to his body, and thus jumping from one pot to another, made a delightful spectacle. After watching him for some time to his great amusement, the other

brother went out of the kitchen, found the
rest, and said to them : " I assure you that
Brother Juniper is cooking for a wedding."
The brothers took his words for a joke ; but
Brother Juniper presently lifted his pots from
the fire and rang the bell for the repast.
And as they went in to dinner, he entered
the refectory with all his dishes, his face
crimsoned with fatigue and the heat of the
fire, and said to them all : " Eat well, and
then let us all go to prayer, and let none
think of cooking any more for a while, for I
have cooked dinner enough to-day to last for
a fortnight." And he placed his stew, of
which there was not a pig in all the Roman
province famished enough to have eaten, on
the table before the brothers. But Brother
Juniper praised up his cooking, to give them
an appetite ; and seeing that the brothers
ate nothing, he said : " Now such fowls as
these are comforting food for the brain, and
such a stew as this will strengthen your
bodies, it is so good." And the brothers
remained lost in devout astonishment at
Brother Juniper's piety and simplicity.

But the guardian, annoyed at such
stupidity and so much waste of good food,
reproved him with great severity. Then
Brother Juniper all at once threw himself
on the ground on his knees before the
guardian, and acknowledged his fault
against him and against all the brothers,
saying : " I am the worst of men ; such a
one commits such a crime and has his eyes

s

put out for it, but I deserve it much more; another is hanged for his faults, but I am more deserving of it for my evil deeds, who am always wasting the good things of God and of the order." And thus sorrowfully he went away, and would not appear before any of the brothers all that day. But when he was gone, the guardian said: "Well-beloved brothers, I would that every day this brother of ours spoilt as many good things as to-day if we had them, solely for our own edification; for out of his great simplicity and charity he has done it all."

How Brother Juniper went to Assisi, once on a time, for his own Confusion

WHILST Brother Juniper was staying once in the valley of Spoleto, he heard of a great solemnity then going on at Assisi, at which a great number of people were assisting with much devotion, and the wish came to him to assist at it also. And behold, he stripped himself of all but his breeches, and thus he went his way, passing through Spoleto and right through the middle of the city, and so arrived at the convent. The brothers, much put out and scandalized at his appearance, rebuked him sharply, calling him foolish and imbecile and reproaching him with bringing confusion on the whole order of St Francis, and wanted to chain him up as a madman. And the general also, who was then at the convent,

called him up before all the brothers, and
in the presence of the whole community
gave him a stern and severe reproof. And
after many words of vigorous indignation,
he said to him : " The nature of your fault is
such, and so great, that I know not what
penance to impose on you." Then said
Brother Juniper, as one who delighted in
his own confusion : " My father, I will tell
thee: let me, for penance, return to the
place whence I came to this feast in the
same manner that I came here."

How Brother Juniper was ravished in spirit
during the celebration of the Mass

AS Brother Juniper was one day hearing
Mass with much devotion, he was ravished
through the elevation of his mind for a long
time. And being left alone and far from
the brothers, as soon as he came to himself
he began thus to say, with great fervour :
" O my brothers, who is there in this world
so exalted that he would not willingly carry
a basket of dung upon his back if there
were given him for it a house full of gold ?
Alas, why are we unwilling to carry a little
shame in order that we may attain to the
blessed life ? "

Of the Sadness which Brother Juniper felt
at the death of his companion, Brother
Amazialbene

BROTHER JUNIPER had a companion whom
he loved intimately, whose name was
Amazialbene; one who possessed the virtue
of patience and obedience in the highest
degree; insomuch that if he had been beaten
all day long he would neither have complained nor protested with a single word.
He was often sent to houses where the
communities were ill-disposed in their conversation, in which he received much perse-
cution, all of which he bore most patiently
without a word of complaint. According
to the bidding of Brother Juniper, he wept
or laughed. And at last he died, as it
pleased God, in the best repute.

When Brother Juniper heard of his
death, it gave him such sadness of mind as
never in his life he had suffered before
through any exterior cause. And thus he
showed with outward signs the great bitter-
ness of soul within him, saying: "Woe is
me to whom now remains no good thing;
and all the world is become distasteful to
me through the death of my sweet and
beloved Brother Amazialbene!" And he
said: "If it were not that the brothers
would give me no peace afterwards, I would
go to his grave and take up his head, and
of the skull I would make two vessels; one
of which I would always eat out of in his

memory and in my devotion, and the other I would drink out of when athirst."

❦

Of the Hand which Brother Juniper saw in the air above him

BROTHER JUNIPER being one day at his prayers, and, perhaps, thinking of his good works, there appeared to him a hand up in the air, and with his bodily ears he heard a voice saying to him: "Brother Juniper, with that hand thou canst do nothing." At which he rose with haste, and lifting and directing steadfastly his eyes to heaven, said with a loud voice, running all the while through the convent: "It is indeed true; it is indeed true." And this he continued to repeat for a considerable time.

❦

The Example of Brother Leo, when St Francis commanded him to wash the Stone

As St Francis was speaking with Brother Leo one day on Mount Alvernia, he said to him: "Brother Little Sheep, wash this stone with water." And forthwith Brother Leo fetched water and washed it. With great joy and delight St Francis said: "Wash it with wine;" and he did so. "Wash it," said St Francis again, "with oil;" and this also was done. Then said St Francis: "Brother Little Sheep, wash this stone with balsam;" and Brother Leo replied: "O sweet father, how should I have balsam in so wild

a place as this ?" And St Francis said to
him : " Know, Brother Little Sheep of
Christ, that this is the stone on which Christ
sat when once He appeared to me here;
and therefore I bade thee wash it four times
without answering me, because Jesus Christ
promised me four singular graces for my
order. The first is that all who love my
order and the brothers sincerely shall have
the grace of final perseverance, and by the
divine favour make a good end. The second
is that all who persecute this order shall be
notably punished. The third is that no
wicked man, persevering in his wickedness,
shall be able to remain long in the order.
The fourth, that this order shall continue
until the Judgment day."

The Life of Brother Giles

How Brother Giles and three of his Companions were received into the Order of the Friars Minor

As the example of holy men is calculated to excite in the minds of the devout hearer a contempt for transitory joys and to inspire him with the desire of eternal salvation, to the honour of God and of His most revered mother, holy Mary, and for the edification of all who hear me, I will speak concerning the operation of the Holy Spirit in our holy Brother Giles, who, while still in the secular garb, touched by the Holy Spirit of God, began to reflect within himself how he might in all his works please God alone.

About this time St Francis appeared, as a new herald of God, to give the world an example of a saintly life, of holy penance and humility; and two years after his own conversion he was joined by a man of admirable prudence and very rich in worldly goods, called Bernard, and by another named Peter of Catania, both of whom were attracted by the example of St Francis to observe evangelical poverty, to distribute all their temporal goods to the poor for the love of God, and to take to themselves the glory of patience and of evangelical perfection and the habit of the Friars Minor. And with great fervour they promised to observe the rule all the days of their life, and this they did with great perfection.

Eight days after their conversion and the distribution of their goods to the poor, which Brother Giles witnessed, being still in the secular garb, and which excited the admiration of all, the example of these noble cavaliers of Assisi, thus despoiling themselves, so inflamed him with divine love that the next day, being the feast of St George in the year 1209, he went betimes in the morning, as one solicitous about his salvation, to the church of St Gregory, which was close to the convent of St Clare. And when he had finished his prayers, having a great desire to see St Francis, he went towards the lepers' hospital where he was dwelling with Brother Bernard and Brother Peter hidden in a mean and humble cottage. And coming to where two roads met, and not knowing which to take, he directed his prayer to Christ, the best of guides, who led him straight to the cottage.

And as he went, St Francis came out of the wood where he had been in prayer, and came to meet him, wondering wherefore he had come. Whereupon Giles threw himself on the ground, and kneeling at his feet humbly begged that he would receive him as one of his companions for the love of God. Then St Francis looking upon him, and seeing his devout aspect, answered and said to him : "Most beloved brother, God has given thee a great grace. If the emperor came to

Assisi and desired to make one of the citizens
a knight of his court or private chamberlain,
ought not such a one to rejoice greatly ? How
much more oughtest thou not to rejoice that
God has elected thee for His knight and beloved servant, to observe the perfect rule of
the Holy Gospel ? And therefore stand firm
and constant in the vocation to which God
hath called thee." And he took him by the
hand and raised him up, and led him into the
aforesaid little house, and called Brother
Bernard, and said to him : " The Lord has
sent us here a good brother, for whom we
shall all rejoice in the Lord ; let us eat together in charity."

And having eaten that which they had in
the hut, St Francis went with Giles to Assisi
to procure cloth to make the habit for the new
brother. And on the way they met a poor
woman, who asked them for alms for the love
of God ; and not knowing how to provide for
the poor woman St Francis turned to Brother
Giles, and with an angelic face said to him :
" For the love of God, dearest brother, let us
give this mantle to the poor woman." And
Brother Giles obeyed the holy father so joyfully that it seemed to him he saw this alms
fly swiftly up to heaven, and in spirit he flew
straight into heaven with it, whence he felt
within himself an unspeakable joy and
renewal of heart. St Francis having
procured the cloth and made the habit, received Brother Giles into the order, who
became in the contemplative life one of the

most glorious religious the world had ever seen.

Immediately after the reception of Brother Giles, St Francis went with him to the province of Ancona, singing with him as they went, and magnifying and praising the Lord of heaven and earth. And he said to Brother Giles : "Son, our order shall be like to the fisherman who casts his nets into the water and catches a multitude of fishes and keeps the larger ones, leaving the small ones in the water." Brother Giles marvelled at this prophecy, because there were in the order as yet only three brothers and St Francis, and up to this time St Francis had not preached publicly, but only as he went along the way admonished and reproved the people, both men and women, saying to them with simplicity and affection : " Love and fear God, and do worthy penance for your sins." And Brother Giles said : " Do that which my spiritual father says to you, because he speaks right well."

How Brother Giles went to St James's in Galicia

AFTER a time, by permission of St Francis, Brother Giles went once to visit the church of St James the Great, in Galicia ; and during the whole journey only once did he take something to eat, on account of the great dearth which then prevailed in all that country. For once, as he went along asking alms and finding no one to give him any charity, it chanced that in the evening he halted by a threshing floor, where there yet remained some unthreshed beans ; these he gathered up and made his supper on them, and there he slept that night, because he willingly sojourned in places solitary and remote from men, that he might the better give himself to vigil and prayer. And he was so much refreshed by God in this supper that he could not have thought it possible to receive such refection had he eaten of divers dishes.

And as he went further on his way, he met on the road a beggar, who asked him for alms for the love of God. And Brother Giles in his charity, having nothing but the habit he wore, cut the hood away from his old mantle and gave it to the poor man for the love of God; and thus for twenty days he journeyed on without a hood. And as he returned through Lombardy, a man called to him, to whom he went readily enough, thinking to receive an alms of him; but as he stretched out his hand, the other placed in it a couple of dice, inviting him to play. And Brother Giles, replying humbly, "God forgive thee, son," went on his way. And thus he went through the world, receiving much contempt and taking it all peacefully.

Of the Manner in which Brother Giles lived
when he went to the Holy Sepulchre

BROTHER GILES went, with the permission
of St Francis, to visit the Holy Sepulchre of
Christ, and got as far as the port of Brindisi,
and there he was detained several days because there was no ship ready. And he,
wishing to live by his own toil, bought a
pitcher, and filled it with water, and went
about the town crying : "Who will have
water ?" And by his toil he earned his
bread and what was necessary for the life of
his body for himself and his companion ; and
afterwards he crossed the sea and visited the
Holy Sepulchre and the other holy places
with great devotion.

And on his way back he was detained
in the city of Ancona for several days ; and
because he was accustomed to live by the
labour of his hands, he made baskets of
rushes and sold them, not for money but for
bread for himself and his companion, and
for the same hire he also carried the dead to
the cemetery. And when this failed him he
returned to the table of Jesus Christ, begging
alms from door to door ; and thus, with
much toil and poverty, went back to St Mary
of the Angels.

How Brother Giles praised Obedience more
than Prayer

A CERTAIN brother was one day praying in
his cell when his guardian sent word to him
that he should go and seek alms by obedience. Whereupon he went immediately to
Brother Giles, and said: "My father, I was
at prayer, and the guardian has commanded
me to go and seek for bread, but it seems to
me better that I should remain at my
prayers." But Brother Giles answered him:
"My son, hast thou not yet known or understood what manner of thing prayer is? True
prayer is to do the will of your superior; and
it is a sign of great pride in one who has
placed his neck under the yoke of holy
obedience when for any reason whatever he
infringes it, thinking thereby to act more
perfectly. The religious who is perfectly
obedient is like a rider mounted on a powerful horse, through whose strength he will
pass fearlessly along the road; and on the
contrary, the disobedient, complaining and
unwilling religious is like one who should
be mounted on a lean, infirm and vicious
horse, for through a little fatigue he will
drop behind and be slain or taken by his
enemies. I tell thee that if a man had so
great devotion and elevation of mind as to
converse with angels, and whilst he thus
conversed he should be called away by one
set over him, he ought at once to leave the
converse of the angels and obey his Superior."

How Brother Giles lived by the Labour of his hands

BROTHER GILES was for a time in a convent in Rome; and according to his custom ever since he entered the order he would live only by his own bodily labour. And this was his manner of life : Early in the morning he heard Mass with much devotion; then he went into the wood which was eight miles from the city of Rome, whence he would gather and carry on his back a faggot of wood, and this he sold for bread and other necessaries.

On one occasion, as he was returning with a load of wood, a woman asked to buy it; and having made their bargain for the price, he carried it to her house. The woman, notwithstanding the bargain agreed upon, seeing that he was a friar, gave him more than she had promised. Then said Brother Giles: "Good woman, I desire not to be overcome by the vice of avarice; therefore I will have no greater price than the bargain I made with thee." And thereupon not only would he take no more than the price agreed upon, but he left the half of it, and departed; at which the woman was inspired with a great devotion towards him.

Brother Giles did all his work in the same spirit of scrupulous honesty. He assisted in shaking down the olives and gathering the grapes. One day, when he was in the market-place, a man was enquiring for someone to beat down his walnuts, and asking another to do it at a certain price; but the other excused himself, on account of the length of the way, and because the walnut trees were very hard to climb. Then said Brother Giles: " Friend, if thou givest me a part of the nuts, I will go with thee to beat them;" and having made this agreement, he went with the man, and, first making the sign of the most holy Cross, with great fear he climbed the walnut tree and began to beat. And when he had done beating, the share that fell to him was so large that he could not carry it in his lap. Wherefore, taking off his habit and tying together the sleeves and the hood, he made a sack of it; and his habit, thus full of nuts, he placed on his back and carried it into Rome, where with great joy he gave all the nuts away to the poor for the love of God. When the sickle was put into the corn, Brother Giles went with the rest of the poor to glean the ears; and if any gave him a handful of grain, he said: "Brother, I have no granary where I could store it;" and for the most part he gave away the ears he gathered, for the love of God.

Rarely did Brother Giles assist in these labours during the whole of the day, because he made it his bargain to have sufficient time to say the canonical hours, and not to fail in making his meditations. On one occasion he went to the fountain of St Sixtus to draw water for the monks with whom he sojourned, and a man asked him for a drink. But

Brother Giles answered : " And how shall I
carry the vessel half emptied to the monks ? "
The other, much offended, gave him many
bad words and hard names ; and Brother
Giles returned to the monks greatly grieved.
Then, borrowing a large vessel, he went
quickly back to the fountain for more water,
and found the man, and said : " Friend, take
and drink as much as thy soul desires, and
be not angry, for to me it seemed unbecom-
ing to carry a vessel half emptied to those
holy monks." Then the man repenting, and
constrained by the charity and humility of
Brother Giles, acknowledged his fault, and
from that hour held him in great veneration.

How Brother Giles was miraculously aided in a
great Necessity

WHILST Brother Giles was in Rome, staying
at the house of a cardinal, as the time of the
great lenten fast drew near, finding he
could not have that quiet of mind he desired, he said to the cardinal : " My father,
with your permission, for my greater peace,
I would pass the Lent with my companion,
in some solitary place." The cardinal answered him : " Well, my dearest brother,
and whither would you go ? The dearth in
these parts is great, and you know the country but little ; let it please you to remain in
my palace, since to me it is a singular grace
to provide you with all you need for the
love of God." Nevertheless, Brother Giles

resolved to go. And he departed from Rome, and went to a high mountain, where formerly there was a castle, and where there still remained a deserted church dedicated to St Lawrence; and therein he took up his abode with his companion, and devoted himself to constant prayer and meditation. They were unknown, and therefore little reverence or charity was shown them, so that they suffered great privations; and in addition, there was a heavy fall of snow, which lasted several days.

And as they could not go outside the church, and no one sent them anything to eat, they remained fasting for three days. Then Brother Giles, seeing he could neither work for their bread nor go out to seek alms, said to his companion: " My dearest brother, let us cry to our Lord with a loud voice that His compassion may provide for us in this extreme necessity, for many monks, being in great need, have cried to God, and His Divine Providence has supplied their wants." Therefore after this example they betook themselves to prayer, entreating God with all their hearts that He would send them relief in their great necessity. Then God, who is all-pitiful, looked upon their faith and devotion, and the simplicity and fervour which had led them thither. A man who was looking towards the church said within himself: " Perchance there may be some good soul in that church doing penance and, on account of the continuance of the snow, without means of living, who may therefore die of want." And inspired by the Holy Spirit, he said: "Yes, I will go and see whether my thought is true or not." And he took bread and a bottle of wine, and went forth; and with great difficulty he arrived at the church, where he found Brother Giles and his companion praying most fervently, and so emaciated with hunger that they had more the appearance of dead men than of living. He had great compassion on them, and, after refreshing and comforting them, returned and told his neighbours of the extremity in which he found the brothers, and begged for the love of God that they would provide for them; whence many, after his example, carried them bread and wine and other things they had need of, for the love of God; and they arranged amongst themselves to provide for all their necessities during the whole of Lent. And Brother Giles, considering their charity and the great mercy of God, said to his companion: "Dearest brother, only just now we prayed to God to provide for us in our need, and He hath heard us; therefore it is meet that we should give Him thanks and praise, and pray for those who have succoured us with their alms, and for all Christian people." And for the great fervour and devotion they had, God gave to Brother Giles such grace that many through his example gave up this evil

world ; and many others, who were not disposed for the religious life, did great penance for their sins within their own homes.

✻

How a Holy Man, whilst at his Prayers, saw
the Soul of Brother Giles enter into Life
eternal

A CERTAIN holy man, who was engaged in
prayer when Brother Giles passed from this
life, beheld his soul, with a great multitude
of other souls, coming out of purgatory and
ascending into heaven; and he saw Jesus
Christ with a multitude of angels come forth
to meet the soul of Brother Giles, who with
all the other souls ascended with sweetest
melody into the glory of paradise.

✻

How, by the merits of Brother Giles, the Soul
of the Friend of a certain Friar Preacher
was delivered from the pains of Purgatory

WHEN Brother Giles was taken sick, a few
days before he died, a Dominican friar was
sick unto death also ; and this friar had a
friend, a friar like himself, who, seeing his
death approaching, said to him : "My
brother, I would, if God would permit, that
after thy death thou return and tell me in
what state thou art." And the sick man
promised to return if it were possible ; and
he died on the same day as Brother Giles.

And after his death he appeared to the
other Friar Preacher, and said : "It was

the will of God that I should keep my promise to thee." Then said the living friar to the dead : "How is it with thee?" And the dead replied : " It is well, because I died on the day on which a holy Friar Minor named Giles passed from this life also, to whom, for his great sanctity, Jesus Christ granted that he should lead all the souls then in purgatory, amongst whom was I in great torment, unto the glory of paradise; and by the merits of this holy Brother Giles I was set free." And having thus spoken, he immediately disappeared; and this other friar revealed the vision to no one. But presently he sickened also; and immediately feared that God had thus punished him because he had not revealed the virtue and the glory of Brother Giles; he asked to see the Friars Minor, and there came to him five couples; and he called together the Friars Preachers with them, and with great earnestness revealed to them the aforesaid vision; and when they had diligently inquired, they found it was even as he said, that on one and the same day the two had passed together from this life.

How God gave special Graces to Brother Giles, and of the year of his Death

BROTHER BONAVENTURE of Bagnioreggio used to say of Brother Giles that God had granted special graces to him for all those

who with devout minds recommended themselves to him in those things which concerned the salvation of their souls.   He
worked many miracles both in his life and
after his death, even as it appears in the
legend, and passed from this life into the
supernal glory in the year of our Lord
twelve hundred and fifty-two, on the feast
of St George, and is buried at Perugia in
the convent of the Friars Minor.

Printed in the United States
153637LV00004B/104/A